Next-Generation Telecom Provisioning AI-Driven, Cloud-Native Architectures for Autonomous Networks

Henry Cyril

Uday Poranki

Made with ❤ on the Notion Press Platform

www.notionpress.com

Preface

Telecommunications networks are undergoing a fundamental architectural transformation driven by the transition to 5G Standalone, the adoption of cloud-native and software-defined infrastructures, and the early emergence of 6G as an AI-native communication paradigm. These developments are reshaping not only the access and core networks, but also the operational and business platforms responsible for service provisioning, assurance, and lifecycle management.

Telecom provisioning systems, traditionally implemented as tightly coupled and sequential workflows within monolithic OSS/BSS platforms, were designed for relatively static services and human-driven operations. In modern networks, however, provisioning must support highly dynamic service models, network slicing, edge computing, massive device connectivity, and stringent service-level guarantees. The scale, concurrency, and real-time requirements of these environments expose fundamental limitations in legacy architectures based on batch processing, synchronous orchestration, and manual intervention.

This book addresses the architectural evolution required to overcome these limitations. It presents a systematic exploration of next-generation telecom provisioning systems built on cloud-native, event-driven, and AI-enabled principles. Provisioning is treated not as a peripheral OSS function, but as a core control plane that integrates distributed systems, real-time data processing, automation, and intelligence across the full-service lifecycle.

The material in this book is informed by both large-scale industry practice and peer-reviewed research. The architectural patterns discussed—event-driven workflows, transaction serialization, idempotent service execution, intelligent queuing, and closed-loop automation— are motivated by real operational challenges observed in Tier-1 telecommunications environments. These challenges include maintaining consistency under extreme concurrency, Page | ii ensuring resilience during partial failures, minimizing service fallout, and enabling autonomous recovery in highly distributed systems.

A central theme of the book is the progression from reactive operations to autonomous networks. As network complexity increases, manual and rule-based operational models become unsustainable. Artificial intelligence, when embedded directly into provisioning and assurance workflows, enables predictive analysis, adaptive control, and self-healing behavior. This work examines how such capabilities can be architecturally integrated to support scalable, resilient, and intent-driven network operations.

The book is intended for researchers, graduate students, and professionals in telecommunications, cloud computing, and distributed systems. It assumes a foundational understanding of networking and software architectures, while emphasizing architectural reasoning and practical applicability. Rather than focusing on specific vendor implementations or evolving standards in isolation, the book highlights enduring design principles that are expected to remain relevant across future generations of telecom networks.

By consolidating architectural insights from cloud-native systems, event-driven design, and AI-enabled automation, this book aims to contribute a coherent framework for understanding and building the provisioning platforms that will underpin autonomous telecom networks in the years ahead.

Dedication

To God, whose guidance and grace made this work possible.

Acknowledgement

The authors express sincere gratitude to God for wisdom, guidance, and perseverance throughout this work. Appreciation is also extended to colleagues and peers for their valuable insights and feedback, and to family members for their constant encouragement, patience, and support.

Contents

Chapter 1: Evolution of Telecom Provisioning Systems

1.1 Chapter Introduction

Chapter 1 is dedicated to the Telecom provisioning systems operation and their evolution. The history of the telecommunications provisioning system is of great technical and historical significance, following the route of manual, semi-manual, and fully automated systems with software-defined networks, which are currently in use. The trend of cutting-edge tech being the sole reason for admiration is no longer the only aspect; rather, the insight revealed by the infrastructure which has been the major factor in turning the world into a global village has changed drastically. The provisioning of a simple telephone line, particularly during the earliest days of telecommunication when electromechanical switches were used, was akin to manual labor, as it involved the use of physical jumper wires on a central distribution frame and manually entering record entries into a variety of siloed record-keeping systems (Heindel & Schlieber, 2002).

The labor-intensive, primitive technique could just be practiced within the confines of a monopoly whose increase in the number of subscribers and the release of new services were quite slow. However, the global deregulation and the advent of digital switches as well as later IP networks made the inefficiencies and high costs of manual provisioning come to the surface like a red tide, much to the dismay of the operators. The demand from the industry was for a system that would be able to handle a volume which was growing at an exponential rate, cut down activation times from weeks to minutes and also manage a more and more complicated range of services, and the cutting-edge software-intensive solutions have made the users' connection to the world an effortless and automatic dance.

1.2 Traditional Telecom Provisioning Models

Telecom service provisioning denotes the series of activities that involve setting up, permitting usage, and providing telecommunication services to either customers or organizations. The allocation of resources such as bandwidth, network connections, and hardware to the user according to their needs is supported by this procedure. The whole process starts with order management, which is essentially the receiving and validating of service requests, then the network components like routers and switches are configured in such a way that the service is available.

When the service is set up, it gets activated and becomes available to the end user. In most cases, continual monitoring is included in provisioning to keep up with the service quality and to handle any issues that may arise. With the increased complexity of networks due to the introduction of 5G and fiber optics technology, service provisioning has changed to the point where it is automated, which results in faster deployment, fewer mistakes, and also scalability (Cyril, 2025).

The process of provisioning telecom services has evolved from simple network service configuration and activation to a very efficient one, powered by agentic workflows of AI. These smart agents change the way provisioning is done by performing repetitive tasks, managing resources in a better way, and supporting decision-making that can change quickly, all of which are automatically done.

The AI agents are very necessary for the monitoring of network conditions and prediction of possible problems to the quality-of-service impact. They mine massive data stones in the search for patterns, thus making the correct configurations and the very fast troubles solving processes. AI in the service activation makes it possible for a smooth coordination among the hardware, software, and the network layers, thus, the activation time is cut down greatly. Besides, the agents can do the real-time tuning which can be optimizing bandwidth in the time of peak usage so that the performance is consistent.

Artificial intelligence automation not only increases scalability but also makes it possible for telecom companies to handle complicated networks such as 5G and even more. The use of AI agents is changing the provisioning process in such a way that it delivers swifter, more reliable, and economical telecom services by reducing human interference and enhancing operational efficiency.

Table 1.1: Traditional vs. Agentic AI Telecom Service Provisioning

Aspect	**Traditional Approach**	**Agentic AI-based Approach**
Data Processing	Manual input and processing	Automated data collection and processing
Speed of Activation	Very slow and often dependent on human input	Real-time activation with minimal delay

Error Rate	Prone to human errors and inconsistencies.	High accuracy through machine learning
Scalability	Limited by human resources and manual processes	Easily scalable across multiple services
Customer Interaction	Reactive support based on complaints	Proactive engagement through automated alerts
Operational Costs	Higher due to manual labor and error correction	Reduced costs through automation

1.2.1 Benefits of AI Agents for Telecom Service Provisioning

- **Efficiency Gains**: By automating processes like network configuration and request processing, AI agents expedite the provisioning process. A 30–40% reduction in activation time enables telecom carriers to manage more service requests with fewer personnel. Faster time-to-market for new services and reduced operating costs are the results of this efficiency.
- **Resource Utilization Optimization**: The network resources are being monitored and optimized in real-time by Resource Management Agents (RMAs). The infrastructure costs can be slashed by as much as 25% through the dynamic resource adjustment in accordance with the demand. This optimization not only prevents overprovisioning but also allows telecom companies to improve their cost efficiency by using resources only when they are actually needed.
- **Proactive Network Management**: Self-healing agents (SHAs) proactively manage the network and, thus, service disruptions can be up to 50% less. The agents not only reroute the traffic or re-provision the network elements automatically but also, minimize the downtime and the cost that goes with manual recovery, giving rise to better service reliability and less maintenance cost.
- **Scalability and Speed**: The implementation of AI bots has made it possible for the telecommunications operators to easily and quickly expand their networks in accordance with the varying demand, especially during busy hours or when introducing new services. Consequently, the service launch is done in a maximum of 40% less time in comparison to

old-fashioned techniques, which consequently allows telecommunication firms to instantly take advantage of new market opportunities.

- **Customer Experience Improvement**: The automation of service requests, provisioning, and billing by AI agents can lead to an increase in customer satisfaction by as much as 30%. The user experience is significantly improved as a result of faster service activation, more accurate billing, and fewer interruptions in service, which in turn promotes loyalty and reduces churn.

1.2.2 Key Differences Between TaaS and Traditional Telecom

Let's take a technical look at it. These variations have an impact on control, speed, support, and cost.

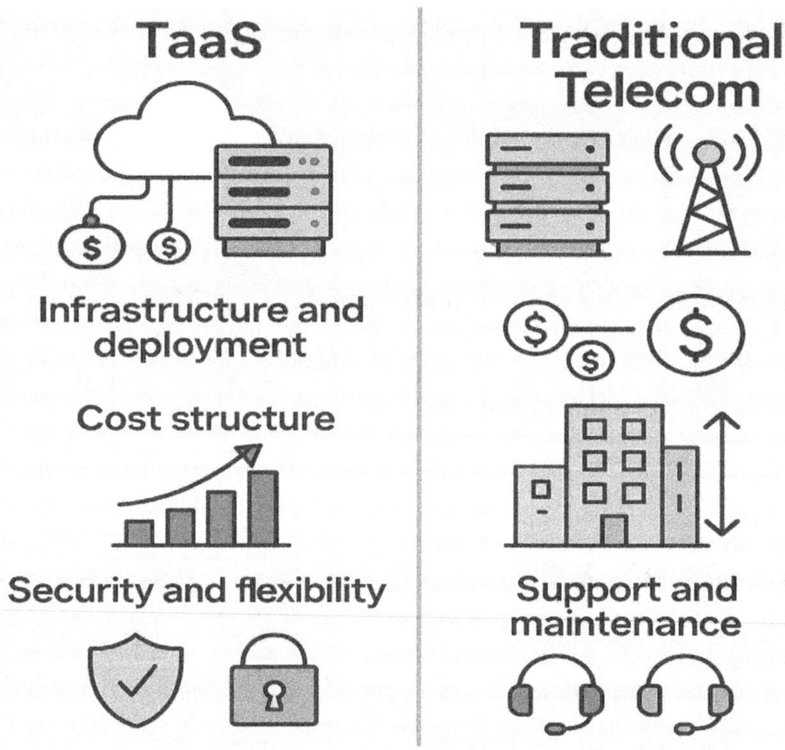

Figure 1.1: Taas vs traditional Telecom

Source: (Spenza, 2025)

- **Infrastructure and Deployment**

Conventional telecommunications systems depend on physical structures such as wires, racks, switchboards, and PBX machines. The full procedure can last for weeks or even months in some cases. One has to order, install, configure, and test the system.

Everything is hosted on the cloud when using TaaS. Virtual phone systems and network services are made available to you, and they are often set up on the same day. There are fewer installation agreements, no disruptions, and no technicians on site.

Here's a table comparing both models:

Table 1.2: Comparison Between Telecommunications as a Service (TaaS) and Traditional Telecom Systems

Feature	TaaS	Traditional Telecom
Hardware	None needed	Required (PBX, switches, phones)
Deployment Time	Same day or within hours	Weeks or months
Installation	Remote/automated	Manual and on-site
Setup Cost	Very low	High upfront investment
Remote Work Support	Built-in	Requires VPNs and extra setup

- **Cost Structure**

The subscription-based pricing model is implemented by TaaS. Only what you use will be charged to you. Spending on telecom is transferred from CapEx to OpEx. For businesses with seasonal peaks or varying staffing levels, this strategy is perfect.

The telecoms world still operates on the fixed pricing model. It does not matter if you use it or not, you pay for the whole package. Long-term contracts are usual. There is an initial high cost for hardware. Maintenance contributes to the expenses.

The cost comparison of TaaS versus Traditional Telecom indicates that TaaS is more flexible and better in budgeting.

- **Scalability and Flexibility**

Scaling a conventional telephone system can imply purchasing new hardware, rewiring, and perhaps even upgrading the physical infrastructure, making the process sluggish and expensive.

TaaS on the other hand, is very flexible as the user, services, or even the location can be added or removed within minutes. The difference between cloud telecom and on-premise models is very clear. It is an ideal solution for companies that are expanding or have remote teams.

Moreover, TaaS brings usage analytics as its added advantage. It allows the customer to know the calling pattern of the employees in terms of who is calling whom, at what time and how frequently. Further, the customer can implement the required changes instantly.

- **Security and Compliance**

A lot of people think that due to the in-house efficiency, traditional systems are the most secure ones. But on the other hand, the management of firewalls, encryption, and access is really complicated and one breach can compromise the whole network.

Most of the TaaS providers follow international standards such as SOC 2, ISO 27001, and HIPAA, for example, the very high standard of security. They also have up-to-date software at all times, and provide services like encrypting voice calls and login with a secondary security check. You are going to enjoy the security of large-scale enterprise-level without the burden of hiring a security team.

Despite giving up hardware control, you will, however, be receiving constant updates and better compliance.

- **Support and Maintenance**

In classic telecom, support is managed either by your IT staff or by the vendor. Repairing takes time. Unrepaired malfunctioning equipment leads to the loss of productivity.

TaaS gives you the option of including support as part of your package. The majority of suppliers provide round-the-clock ticketing, phone, and chat support. You are not responsible for server repairs, they are. This results in fewer interruptions for you.

Moreover, one of the drawbacks of traditional telecom is the use of old technology. Even now, a lot of firms are still using PBX hardware that dates back to the early 2000s.

If you want to know whether you are one of the companies that overpay lately without noticing, then you should learn about these billing errors that many firms still make in 2025.

1.2.3 Pros and Cons of Traditional Telecom

By the year 2025, a good number of businesses will have remained faithful to classic telecom systems. The following are the reasons for that as well as the justification for others moving in a different direction.

Pros

- Reliable and steady
- Internal network management
- Dependable for operations in a fixed site
- Frequently combined with additional office services

Cons

- High setup and upkeep costs
- Extended contract durations
- Outdated hardware
- Slow to scale
- Fewer features and personalized choices
- Unsuitable for distant work

Not only did twelve main telecom companies from Europe inform about the 6G technology dilemma caused by insufficient spectrum, but also the need for radical modifications in the old telecom systems highlighted by this issue.

1.3 Shift Toward Intelligent Network Provisioning

The telecommunications industry, which is changing at a fast pace, has seen the emergence of an advanced intelligent network (AIN) as one of the main factors behind its continuous innovations and increased efficiency. AIN is a complex system that supports various telecommunications services, including traditional voice and data ones, but is not limited to them only. AIN is transforming how we work, communicate, and engage with technology by incorporating cutting-edge technologies like artificial intelligence, machine learning, and data analytics.

One kind of provisioning. The network component that enables the service and permits the client to utilize it must be supplied for the services that are assigned to the customer in the customer relationship management (CRM). Services like Microsoft Media Server (mms://) might be enabled by several network elements, therefore the link between a service defined in the CRM and a service on the network elements is not always one-to-one.

The service mediation device transforms the service and its associated parameters to one or more services and parameters on the relevant network elements during provisioning. Provisioning logic is the algorithm that converts a system service into network services.

The telecom expense management (TEM) software's core can automatically receive electronic invoice feeds from your carriers, and it can instantly audit every single line-item charge all the way down to the User Support and Operations Center (USOC) level. Each circuit number supplied by each of your carriers will be recorded by the provisioning software. If billing takes place outside of the agreed-upon rate, an exception rule will raise a red flag and alert the designated staff person to investigate the billing problem.

AIN leverages a modular and flexible architecture, allowing network operators to quickly deploy and manage a wide array of services. The range of services offered varies from the simple ones such as giving the option to forward calls or leave messages to the complicated ones including forecasting customer behavior through data and providing assistance via non-human agents. AIN makes possible to have instant decisions and flexible service provisioning which are very vital for satisfying the requirements of the modern world that changes quickly in terms of technology and communication.

Automated provisioning refers to the capability of delivering IT or telecom services through automated procedures that are preconfigured and do not need human involvement. It is a kind of principle of design that allows the whole automation process supported by specifications, policies, and analytics to be implemented easily.

Network provisioning is a very important step for the companies to let the allowed users, machines, and servers enter their network. It consists of the areas of both connectivity and security, such as creating users for Wi-Fi, installing software, giving IP addresses, and setting up firewalls. If you are going to provision your network properly, then it will not only enhance the efficiency of employees but also the security and thus make your firm's cyber security stronger.

1.3.1 Key components of network provisioning

Automated network provisioning is a process that involves the utilization of various components and technologies that, when combined, can effectively manage the installation and setup of network devices.

- **DHCP (Dynamic Host Configuration Protocol)**

In larger organizational networks, DHCP server is within the major services providing the automatic IP address to the devices connected to the network. In a device provisioning scenario, the device gets its IP from the DHCP server dynamically along with the instruction for downloading the initial configuration and software thus avoiding any manual pre-configuration.

- **Orchestration platforms and tools**

Configuration management tools are responsible for the automation of the whole process of defining, deploying, and monitoring configuration changes for network devices. Solutions of this type, for instance, Cisco CrossWorks Network Services Orchestrator (NSO) for switches and routers or Palo Alto Panorama for built-in Palo Alto firewalls, make it possible for network administrators to have configuration consistency, compliance both enforced, and updates done throughout the entire distributed network infrastructure.

Automation tools such as Ansible, Puppet, or Chef allow administrators to set up provisioning policies, templates, and workflows in a declarative way and distribute them to the devices through the push method.

- **Automation scripts and templates**

Automation scripts are used for device configuration. These scripts can be customized to suit the specific requirements of an organization, enabling efficient deployment and configuration of device initialization, VLAN configuration, and access control policies of network devices. By standardizing configuration templates and using version control systems like Git, administrators can ensure consistency and repeatability in their provisioning workflows.

- **Source of Truth**

All scripts, automation templates, and workflows are stored in a version control system like Git. This ensures that all new deployments can be executed on the latest version of the code. If there is a need to add support for a new feature any changes should be made with the same approach as the software life cycle and be thoroughly reviewed and tested before its deployment. More information on sources of truth can be found here, in our previous Source of Truth vs. Source of Intent in network automation article.

1.3.2 Benefits of Network Provisioning

When done correctly, network provisioning provides enhanced security, as only approved users and devices can access your company's sensitive systems and data. This reduces the risks associated with digital systems and mitigates potential cyber threats. Other network provisioning benefits include:

- **Streamlined Workflows:** Proper network provisioning is also a factor that can affect employee workflows positively. When people working on the same project have the necessary tools for their positions, they can do their work quickly and without any interruptions or irritation.
- **Improved Compliance:** A properly set up network not only aids in keeping up with the industry's rules regarding security, accessibility, and other matters but also provides the necessary infrastructure. The regulatory requirements will be met and maintained through the digital environment created by your IT team, which will be assisted by the controls that were put in place during provisioning.
- **Centralized Data Management:** All networking data accessible to various agencies is stored in a centralized database.
- **Automation:** When you have automated processes, it cuts manual input and reduces potential human errors.
- **Vendor and Carrier Integration:** Ensure the seamless integration with suppliers and carriers to make the business operate more effectively and less complex.
- **Efficiency and Cost Savings:** Automated provisioning genuinely enhances operational efficiency, lessens waiting periods, and costs less money.

Network provisioning for the telecom sector plays a critical role in keeping the operations running smoothly, improving the customers' experience, and increasing the company's revenues. Call ETI Software to learn more about its network provisioning solutions and see how they enable telecom providers to deliver exceptional service while reducing costs and improving overall performance.

1.3.3 Types of network provisioning

1. Server provisioning

A server, whether cloud-based or on-premises, has to be provided with the appropriate data, software, and configuration before it can operate on a network.

The steps in this process typically include:

- Setting up an operating system, device drivers, and tools for partitioning and setup
- Setting up business apps and software
- Configuring IP addresses and other factors
- Installing virtualization software or partitioning
- Establishing Wi-Fi and Ethernet connections, if necessary
- Conducting a system audit to make sure no repairs are required

These provisioning procedures will be carried out via an online interface if the server is cloud-based. Many manufacturers provide solutions for automating the server provisioning process, and Internet service providers (ISPs) and cloud providers frequently offer tools to facilitate server provisioning.

2. Device provisioning

Hardware needs to be setup, checked, secured, and modified before it can be used. Device identification and user identity are always kept apart in workplace networks, even while multiple devices are assigned to particular employees. More flexibility in device deployment, more thorough device management, and improved shared device management are all made possible by this.

3. Internet-access provisioning

In order to connect and activate an Internet gateway, this process starts with a contract with an ISP.

Installing and configuring wireless access points, configuring hardware for firewall software, setting up and securing a cabled or wireless local-area network (LAN), editing software to appropriately include the new LAN, adding the new LAN to network monitoring tools, and testing the systems are additional steps.

4. User provisioning

The IT and HR divisions of a company are involved in user provisioning. Employees must be given corporate identities, hardware, software, database access, and other resources relevant to their responsibilities when they are onboarded, promoted, or moved.

Eliminating such objects once employees leave the organization is equally crucial.

It is crucial to clarify that "users" might refer to contractors, partners, vendors, customers, and employees. In a more general sense, "user" refers to any anyone who needs certain hardware or access to information or programs.

1.3.4 Risks and challenges of automated network provisioning

Despite the fact that automated network provisioning comes with various benefits including increased efficiency, scalability, and automation, its use in the organizations entails risks and challenges that the organizations have to deal with:

- **Security:** Weaknesses in the implementation of provisioning might be abused by the attackers to penetrate the network or to cause denial-of-service (DoS) attacks, thereby leading to unauthorized access to the provisioning servers, compromised device authentication, or even interception of configuration data during transit. It is essential to employ encryption, authentication protocols, and access controls as a deterrent to these threats. If there is no adequate security, someone who has physically accessed the network could easily initiate the provisioning process of their own device and thus get unauthorized access to the network, which in turn, would lead to disruptions in company operations. The situation is not much different when it comes to the interception of configuration data. All sensitive data should be encrypted so that it is impossible to read the configuration files.
- **Configuration errors:** It is essential for the administrators to meticulously check the configuration templates and to set up the validation mechanisms that would be able to detect and correct the errors even before they balloon into critical problems. One option is to perform rigorous testing, and Digital Twins can assist in this case. The article Beyond simulation: the practical applications of Digital Twins in modern networking provides more information on this topic. The automatic provisioning of a misconfigured device can lead to the creation of security holes, stop network activities, or even cause the loss of data integrity.
- **Multi-vendor environment:** Many different vendors, software versions, and hardware capacities can lead to compatibility issues. Standardization efforts, vendor-agnostic provisioning protocols, and interoperability testing are needed to ensure consistent provisioning.

- **Dependency on network connectivity:** Automated network provisioning relies on network connectivity to establish communication between devices and provisioning servers. In environments with unreliable network connectivity, such as remote sites, it may encounter challenges in provisioning devices efficiently. Provisioning multiple devices in one location at the same time may use up bandwidth and cause a slowdown. Implementing a local server to download software or uploading software to the on-site router and then serving it locally to all devices instead of remotely should be considered.
- **Scalability:** The network growth provisioning system must be able to handle an increased workload. Tracking of the deployed configuration and reliably serving all requests must be considered when deploying an orchestration platform.
- **Engineer knowledge:** With the deployment of any new solution in the network one subject that should be always kept in mind is the knowledge and skills of the engineers that are going to implement and manage the solution. Engineers should feel comfortable with deployment, change implementation and troubleshooting of any issues found in the automated network provisioning. Some time out from daily tasks may be required to attend the necessary training.

1.4 Service-Oriented and Policy-Based Provisioning

Service-oriented provisioning and policy-based provisioning are two different, yet complementary, ways of managing and delivering IT resources and capabilities each having its philosophy under the hood and operational benefits. Service-oriented provisioning is a fundamental change in the emphasis of management of the raw infrastructure pieces (such as simply turning internet access on/off or complex profiles) to the definition and supply of particular, reusable services which are explicitly tied to business processes or user requirements. This model is based on the principles of Service-Oriented Architecture (SOA) and enables the service providers to provide a particular set of services as a product portfolio to increase product differentiation and price differentiation on a more granular basis.

In contrast, policy-based provisioning is an architectural approach that is based on high-level rules which are called policies to automate and control the process of service provisioning and resource management. Policies describe the desired behavior, constraints, and quality of service (QoS) requirements rather than manual configuration of each request which are then implemented by an automated system. Dealing with complex and dynamic systems like cloud computing or telecommunication networks that cross different administrative areas, the technique is very important because the resources availability and users' requirements can change very fast.

1.4.1 Service Provisioning in Telecom

Telecommunications services aren't magically there—they go through a careful process called service provisioning. In the end, provisioning is the service provider's means to make your communication tools ready for use in the telecom industry. Provisioning is the process that assures proper operation of the network without errors through configuration, deployment, and management of the entire IT and network infrastructure including hardware, IP addresses, and services. It consists of creating the infrastructure, installing the equipment, licensing the software, creating user accounts, etc., so that everything works perfectly from the very first day.

Provisioning, to put it simply, is the behind-the-scenes setup that arranges everything in such a manner that the telecommunication services, including phone systems and internet, work according to the requirements of the business.

What Is Service Provisioning in Telecom?

Service provisioning means setting up telecom services. It includes the installation of all supporting hardware, software, and network systems for different activities like making and receiving phone calls, voicemail collection and redirection, and internet access, etc.

It can be compared to the core of your communication system. No matter if you are going to use a completely new setup or to make some changes to an old one, the provisioning will take care that all the necessary components are installed, interlinked provided and tailored to the needs of your company.

The provisioning procedure is increasingly often automated using automation technologies. Automation expedites this procedure, lowers mistake rates, and enhances service management.

1.4.2 Components of Service Provisioning

When creating or enhancing a company phone system, a number of components come together. These tools assist in controlling how calls are handled both within and outside of your company.

When your provider is provisioning, they will:

- Establish the destination for incoming calls.
- Direct calls to the appropriate departments or individuals
- Give callers recorded information before they speak with a real person.
- Turn on call forwarding.
- Produce automatic messages
- Configure voicemail
- As part of the provisioning process, configure and oversee every phone or device, including keeping an accurate device inventory.

These provisioning operations guarantee that your phone system functions effectively and meets the everyday demands of your company.

What Is the Difference Between Provisioning and Configuration?

When setting up a telecom system, provisioning and configuration are two connected but distinct phases.

The first step is provisioning. Hardware, software, and network connections have to be prepared and this is called provisioning process and the system is ready for use. At the end of provisioning, the system is already installed and connected. The installation procedure includes checking and getting the details of the endpoint and configuration to guarantee that the installation is done correctly before the next step of configuration is taken. Configuration is then done. This is the period when your phone system is tailored to your particular requirements. This involves configuring features such as:

- Desk phones or softphones (computer or mobile phone applications)
- Voicemail boxes and call groups
- Personalized call flows
- Network configurations that align with your team's communication style

Why Is Provisioning Important?

Because it establishes the framework for everything else, provisioning is crucial. Your communication system could not operate as intended if it is not properly provisioned. Higher client happiness, increased accuracy, and increased efficiency are all advantages of efficient provisioning.

A successful provisioning procedure aids:

- Enhance employee communication within the company
- Make it simpler for clients to connect with the appropriate individuals
- Make sure systems are dependable and safe.
- Lower the possibility of errors or downtime
- Reduce operating expenses by increasing productivity and reducing mistakes
- Encourage upcoming updates and modifications

Every call that your company makes or receives depends on a system that is adequately provided. It's the first step in ensuring that your phone and communication devices continue to function properly.

1.4.3 Policy based provisioning

The policy-based provisioning of telecom is the process through which network services, network resources and subscriber entitlements are automatically configured and controlled according to pre-defined policies, as opposed to manual configuration. The policies are based on subscriber profiles, service plans, SLAs, network conditions and business rules. The network does not require engineers to configure all the services manually, so policy engines such as PCRF (4G) and PCF (5G) dynamically determine who receives what, when and how in real time. This enables the operators to be able to provision data speed, QoS, roaming access, throttling and application prioritization immediately and uniformly throughout the network.

In the contemporary telecommunication networks, the policy-based provisioning has been closely coupled with the components of the core network, the charging systems and orchestration platforms. Policy system provides an automated method by which rules are evaluated and the suitable network behavior is provided when a subscriber is attaching to the network or requesting a service. This allows dynamic activation of services, differentiated user experience, effective resource usage, and fast service rollout. In absence of policy-based provisioning, the telecom networks would degenerate into a life of manual anarchy, reduced service delivery, and unreliable subscriber experience. Of it, in brief, there is the policy, which, as it were, is the brain; and the provisioning, which is the muscle.

1.4.4 Types of Policy-Based Provisioning in Telecom

1. **Subscriber-Based Provisioning:** This type offers network services at the personal level of subscribers. The policies are implemented based on the subscription package, quota, roaming and entitlements to the services by the user. As an example, a premium user can have a better bandwidth and latency than a basic user, whereas a basic user can be limited once he has used enough data. This is the most widespread type of policy-based provisioning and is widely utilized in mobile broadband services.
2. **Service-Based Provisioning:** Service-based provisioning implements policies based on the nature of service being used, e.g. VoLTE, video streaming, IoT, or enterprise VPN. Services vary in terms of performance and quality of service (QoS) needs and policies make sure that bandwidth, priority, and latency are provisioned appropriately. This enables the operators to provide differentiated services using the same physical network without quality and control loss.
3. **Network-Condition-Based Provisioning:** In this case, the policies adjust provisioning dynamically depending on the current network conditions, i.e. congestion, load or failures. The policies can slow down non-critical users during the peak hours or congestion and maintain resources to be used by emergency services or high-priority services. Such a provisioning enhances the network efficiency and eliminates the excessive load of the network due to surges in demand.
4. **Location-Based Provisioning Context-Based Provisioning:** This provisioning type uses policies that are dependent on the location of the user or roaming as well as the access network (4G, 5G, Wi-Fi). As an illustration, roaming users could get limited services, dissimilar charge regulations, or slower speeds. This in 5G is also applied to network slicing, where the various virtual networks are provided by policy depending on the context and use case.

1.5 Automation and Digital Transformation in Telecom

One of the most significant transformations that the telecommunications industry has ever experienced is the widespread adoption of automation and the digital transformation of the industry. The market competition so strong that the need to make an improvement of even slight dimensions is no longer a strategic choice but rather a necessity. The accessibility of seamless and personalized experiences by changing the customers' needs and the fast-paced technological change with 5G, AI, and the IoT are the main factors behind this necessity.

The adoption of new, agile, software-defined, and cloud-native platforms instead of old hardware-driven and legacy operations and infrastructures has changed the phone companies' ways of functioning and how they generate value. Moving up to this multifaceted change, the telecoms will not only stop to be a company that provides connectivity but will also gradually become a tech-based organization (techcos) with the ability to discover new income sources, greatly improve its operational performance to become a major innovator in a wide range of areas (from healthcare to manufacturing) and, finally, become a key operator in the innovation of other areas (e.g., healthcare, etc.).

1.5.1 Impact of Digital Transformation in Telecom

The telecommunications sector is leading digital transformation, which in turn is a result of fast technology developments, changing customer needs, and an ever more competitive market. Digital transformation in telecommunications has a wider scope than mere technology adoption, as it entails the transformation of the various business aspects, the enhancement of the operational efficiency and the customer experience as well.

5G, AI, cloud computing, and IoT are all new technologies that are forcing the telecom industry to adapt in order to maintain their lead. Telecom digitalization brings new services—the operators can now offer high-speed connectivity, apply automation, and manage services intelligently—, the traditional voice and data are still there. Digital transformation opens up new opportunities for telecom players to enhance their infrastructures, decrease their operational costs, and come up with new services that are in line with the constantly changing business and consumer needs.

Telecoms that overall and are teles services b digital transformation can save a lot of money on the operation up to 30% and the quality of services will be delivered 40% faster than before according to the industry reports. These numbers are the reason why digital transformation in telecom is not anymore, an option but a must for survival in the competitive telecom landscape.

Telecom Industry Disruption: How Digital Technologies are Reshaping the Sector

The deployment of digital technologies has caused a radical change in the telecom industry. The old, conventional models that had the characteristic of heavy infrastructure and small service offerings are now gradually being replaced by the widely-used, virtualized deploying networks that support dynamic scaling of telecom operations. Below are some of the important digital technologies in telecom:

- **Cloud Computing & Virtualization:** The investment by telecos is moving forward with ancient infrastructure to novel concepts. Networks that are jolted with such networks will require high agility-the ability to adapt to market requirements and bear minimal costs.
- **AI & Machine Learning:** The adoption of AI analytics supports the various activities mentioned in the title, notably, the predictions of maintenance, detection of fraud, and more tailored customer experiences.
- **IoT & Edge Computing:** Telecommunications companies take advantage of the Internet of Things (IoT) networks along with edge computing to provide quicker data handling and give instant knowledge.
- **Blockchain for Security & Transparency:** Blockchain increases the security of data, high protection against fraud, and automatic execution of contracts in telecommunications transactions.

Operators can strengthen network performance, cut back known downtimes, and shape more resilient digital ecosystems when these technologies are in place - unusually perceptive though not without occasional uncertainty and bouts of extravagance.

1.5.2 Benefits of Digital Transformation in Telecom

If your telecom company chooses to put a spotlight on digital transformation programs, what can it expect to be the outcome? Here are a couple of the advantages that are pretty much usual.

1. **New business models**

Digital transformation gives power to telecom companies to experiment with new ways of growing them. IoT allows telecom to go into areas such as smart homes and connected cars. For instance, AT&T. They changed their business using AI and the cloud, and one of the services they offered was predictive maintenance.

2. **Revenue growth**

Through diversification of their offerings and market explorations, new income sources along with trend adoption are possible. Cloud infrastructure and cost-cutting are two ways that better profit margins come.

3. **Improved customer experience**

The telecoms are digital transformation taking their services to the next level. They can use AI analytics and automation to personalize their services, forecast customer needs, and troubleshoot rapidly.

As per the report released by McKinsey, a staggering 71% of the people want businesses to treat them individually. Moreover, 76% of the customers feel upset when the opposite occurs. Telecom companies are enhancing their communication with customers through automation of various tasks like billing and providing customers with self-service options.

4. **Streamlined processes**

Transitioning to digital is not only about enhancing customer experience. It is also about improving the efficiency of operations behind the scenes. Telecom companies will be able to automate more of their activities and will be able to perform fewer manual tasks. For instance, through the use of network management tools that are connected to each other, telecoms can observe their infrastructure constantly from any place.

1.5.3 Automation in Telecom

Telcos are turning AI and automation into their strategic top positions, given the new network difficulties and the need to remedy their revenue decline. This paper points out the methods of telcos for automation and suggests the gradual transition from short-term intra-process automation to long-term inter-process automation as the right way to go.

Automation will become one of the major factors that help telcos to stand out in the market which is getting more and more saturated day by day, thus creating a competitive differentiation. In case the telcos are focusing on offering the best connectivity, or they are attempting to be more than just connectivity providers, they will still have to rely on automation of their network and service operations to cope with the problem of declining revenues caused by network commoditization.

Why do telcos need automation?

Seventy percent of those who responded to our poll said they planned to go beyond just basic connection and were looking for new ways to increase income. Telcos are increasingly looking to take use of cutting-edge technologies like edge computing and 5G to provide customers with unique solutions, especially in the B2B2X market. Regardless of their strategic approach, network and service automation will be a crucial enabler for all telcos to overcome falling revenue growth.

Figure 1.2: Automation for telcos, new avenues for revenue growth

Source: (Jamnadass, 2021)

Telcos must develop a plan for expanding automation in their network and service operations in order to retain cost savings, manage growing network complexity (with 5G), and offer robust connection. More intelligent automated procedures (that make use of AI/ML) will be a crucial enabler for telcos looking to take use of new technologies; they will find it difficult to handle growing complexity with manual operations:

- **Network operations:** To handle growing complexity on the network side, use cases like network maintenance, defect detection, self-optimization, and CI/CD will be crucial. For instance, telcos may need to manage network services across different locations (e.g. via edge computing).
- **Service operations:** Use cases including customer and partner management, service delivery, and service assurance will be crucial facilitators for telcos looking to advance

higher up the value chain to investigate dynamic business models that introduce more complexity.

1.6 Operational Challenges in Legacy Networks

CIOs of large corporations are faced with the neither easy nor pleasant responsibility of making sure their network infrastructure is always adapted to the changing business requirements. Outdated networks, that are commonly based on old technologies, are the main source of the problems that very often lead to organizations losing their speed, being less secure, and performing poorly altogether. SD-WAN (Software-Defined Wide Area Networking) is a revolutionary solution that, in a big way, will lift the burden off the enterprises' infrastructure by making them more modern and less complicated.

1.6.1 Challenges of Legacy Networks

- **Limited Scalability and Flexibility:** Legacy networks have a tendency to be inflexible and hard to expand. When companies grow and spread, it can be a hard and expensive process to add new locations or increase the bandwidth. Such a lack of adaptability can hinder creativity and diminish the pace at which business operations can go on.
- **High Operational Costs:** Costly processes like maintaining and managing legacy networks are partly due to the hardware-heavy characteristic of these networks which needs a great deal of investing in the physical infrastructure, not to mention, the reoccurring maintenance and support fees. Complexity of managing numerous network devices may also contribute to rising operational costs.
- **Security Vulnerabilities:** Legacy networks are at higher risk of unhealthy interventions since the security technologies used are much older and control is not exercised in a centralized manner. Relying on legacy systems as a security measure will not only expose the enterprises to more sophisticated cyber-attacks, but will also endanger the leaking of sensitive information.
- **Performance Bottlenecks:** The performance of traditional WAN architectures across the board has been inconsistent mostly due to the use of cloud apps and the presence of remote workers. These factors have negatively affected the user experience through delays, packet loss, and jitter, which in turn have severely impacted productivity and customer satisfaction.

- **Complex Management:** Handling a legacy network usually means coming across and having to manage a great variety of different devices and configurations. The resulting complexity can foster inefficiencies and raise the possibility of mistakes by personnel so that the IT department finds it difficult to keep a network running at its best.

1.6.2 SD-WAN: Network Solutions Reimagined

SD-WAN separates the network control plane from the hardware and uses software-defined principles, thus, creating new opportunities for companies who want to improve their digital infrastructure.

- **Enhanced Scalability and Flexibility:** SD-WAN separates the network control plane from the hardware it runs on, and this enables management and orchestration to be done from one place. Thus, it enhances the flexibility of the network and its ability to meet the requirements of the business that might undergo changes. Moreover, there are no limitations in terms of physical infrastructure because the addition of new locations or the raising of bandwidth has become a matter of speed and efficiency.
- **Cost Efficiency:** The expensive MPLS circuits are less depended on thanks to the use of broadband internet and other inexpensive connectivity options with SD-WAN. In turn, this can result in a huge amount of cost savings on both capital and operational expenditures. Moreover, the handled and facilitated management of SD-WAN does not require the presence of specialized IT staff, which is another way of cutting down operational costs.
- **Robust Security:** In-built security functionalities come with SD-WAN solutions like encryption, firewall, and secure segmentation. The centralized control guarantees that there will be uniform security policies all over the network making it less complicated to defend against cyber threats. The advanced capabilities of threat detection and response ensure that the enterprises can rather quickly identify and contain security incidents.
- **Improved Performance:** SD-WAN continuously analyzes the current status of the networks and directs the traffic accordingly, thereby guaranteeing that the most important apps get the required amount of bandwidth and the easiest-to-use paths with the least waiting. The end-user will experience a more reliable and a more consistent user experience, regardless of the location or the nature of the application (cloud or remote).

Application-aware routing and WAN optimization are two of the features that help to further improve performance.

- **Simplified Management:** By means of SD-WAN, centralized and automated network management becomes a reality, thus simplifying the traditional networks' complexity. IT staff can do the network monitoring and management tasks through one screen which is beneficial in the case of updating, troubleshooting and performance maintenance.

1.6.3 Navigating SD-WAN Implementation

A successful SD-WAN deployment is not only a matter of technology but also a matter of aligning that technology with business goals, infrastructure, and capabilities of the organization. It requires a tactical way of thinking that will take into account both the short-term needs and the long-term objectives.

- **Assess Current Network Infrastructure:** Perform a deep evaluation of the current networking situation in order to spot difficulties and enhancements. It will support the creation of an SD-WAN system that is customized to the exact business needs.
- **Define Clear Objectives:** First and foremost, it is essential to define explicit objectives for the SD-WAN implementation, including but not limited to, cost reduction, quality of service enhancement, and security advancement. This will serve as a roadmap for the deployment process and guarantee that it is in sync with the goals of the business.
- **Choose the Right SD-WAN Solution:** Choose an SD-WAN solution that best fits the needs of your organization. Take into account aspects like scalability, security features, management simplicity, and vendor support.
- **Plan for a Phased Deployment:** Implement SD-WAN solution in increments to lessen disturbances and facilitate a seamless switch over. Initially, a pilot project will be launched to check the solution and make required changes prior to deploying it over the whole network.
- **Train IT Staff:** To provide a thorough training for IT personnel so that they can manage and take care of the new SD-WAN infrastructure. It will be a great support in the realization of the deployment advantages to the maximum.

SD-WAN is a win-win solution for CIOs facing the problems of old-fashioned network companies. Not only does SD-WAN make it easier to scale, but it also saves costs, gives strong security, boosts performance, and simplifies management. Thus, SD-WAN can still be the main switch for the whole enterprise infrastructure to advance and be of full benefit to the organizations in the digital era. Over time, technology will develop and enterprises will enjoy even more benefits and added features from their SD-WAN setups.

1.7 Chapter Summary

The development of telecom provisioning from conventional manual and hardware-centric models to intelligent, automated, and service-oriented methods is covered in this chapter. It describes how the adoption of intelligent network management systems and policy-based provisioning has been fueled by growing customer demand and service complexity. The chapter also emphasizes how digital transformation and automation may increase network scalability, service delivery speed, and operational efficiency. Despite these developments, legacy networks still have to deal with operational problems like high maintenance costs, limited flexibility, and integration problems. The necessity of contemporary provisioning frameworks to enable dynamic services and guarantee effective telecom network operations is emphasized throughout the chapter.

Very Short Questions

1. Protocol that assigns IP automatically
2. AI engine in 5G policy control
3. Software-defined wide area network
4. Automated traffic recovery agents
5. Cloud-based telecom model
6. High-level control rules
7. Service transformation logic
8. Virtualized telecom infrastructure
9. Legacy hardware phone system
10. Central configuration repository

Short Questions

1. What is telecom service provisioning?
2. Why did manual provisioning become inefficient over time?
3. What is the main advantage of TaaS over traditional telecom?
4. How does SD-WAN improve network performance?
5. Explain policy-based provisioning in one line.
6. How do AI agents improve network provisioning?
7. What role does orchestration platforms play in provisioning?
8. Why is automated provisioning important for 5G networks?
9. What is the difference between provisioning and configuration?
10. Mention one security risk in automated provisioning.

MCQs (Multiple Choice Questions)

1. **Early telecom provisioning primarily relied on:**
   A. Cloud platforms
   B. AI orchestration
   C. Manual jumper wiring and records
   D. Virtual networks
2. **Agentic AI provisioning mainly improves:**
   A. Hardware lifespan

B. Manual auditing

C. Speed, accuracy, scalability

D. Billing paperwork

3. TaaS stands for:

A. Telecom as Software

B. Technology as Service

C. Telecom as a Service

D. Transmission as System

4. A major disadvantage of legacy networks is:

A. High flexibility

B. Low security risk

C. Performance bottlenecks

D. Easy scalability

5. The major driver behind automated provisioning was:

A. Customer complaints

B. Deregulation and digital networks

C. Social media growth

D. Smartphone usage

6. Policy-based provisioning in 5G uses which component?

A. DHCP

B. PCRF

C. PCF

D. CRM

7. SD-WAN primarily separates:

A. Data and storage

B. Hardware and software licensing

C. Control plane from hardware

D. Voice from data

8. Automated provisioning mainly reduces:

A. Bandwidth

B. Human error

C. Cloud usage

D. Encryption

9. Which protocol dynamically assigns IP addresses?

A. DNS

B. DHCP

C. HTTP

D. FTP

10. Service-oriented provisioning focuses on:

A. Hardware components

B. Business-aligned reusable services

C. Manual configuration

D. Static networks

MCQ Answer sheet

Q1	Q2	Q3	Q4	Q5	Q6	Q7	Q8	Q9	Q10
C	C	C	C	B	C	C	B	B	B

Chapter 2: Cloud-Native Architectures in Telecom Networks

2.1 Chapter Introduction

The adoption of the cloud-native architecture in telecommunications networks is a radical change that will no longer be monolithic systems but will have a more flexible, scalable, and resilient operating paradigm. This change in architecture is not about simply lifting and shifting existing applications to a cloud, but instead re-defining the functionality of network functions so as to take full advantage of the natural characteristics of cloud computing, including on-demand allocation of resources, automation, and distributed processing. It is aimed at making the operations more agile by many times, and Communication Service Providers (CSPs) are able to innovate at a faster rate, satisfy the tough demands of the next-generation services such as 5G (high bandwidth, low latency), and run more cost-efficiently, by making the utilization of resources more effective and automating more complex lifecycle management processes. This shift is vital in an environment where the expectations of customers to be fast, reliable and innovative services are continually increasing.

Simply put, cloud-native telecom network architecture is supported by a number of technological blocks that are aimed at complexity management and high availability. Network functions are decomposed into small, independent, and loosely coupled microservices, and are then bundled into containers (such as those offered as part of Docker) and lightweight portable and consistent, irrespective of their location in a public, private, or hybrid cloud infrastructure. These many containers are deployed and managed via orchestration platforms which are automated with Kubernetes being the standard used in the industry.

2.2 Microservices-Based Telecom Applications

The advent of telecom microservices is hastening the transformation of OSS/BSS management practices and the introduction of new services by telcos in an effort to increase connectivity income. One of the critical features necessary for the successful implementation of microservices is the ability to handle and leverage data obtained from various OSS/BSS. The data platform must not only perform well, but also be scalable in the future—without going over budget, of course.

The idea of microservices architecture is to decompose large information technology systems into smaller, more manageable parts that can carry out specific functions.

The solution with a monolithic design lacks agility, scalability, extensibility, and on-demand capacity, while the microservices approach is superior. Customers in the telecom industry are increasingly demanding a personalized and omnichannel experience, and this is a fantastic tool to help make that a reality.

Microservices typically work with Docker-type platforms, which bundle apps into separate containers that talk to each other through application programming interfaces. In addition to API development, developers with knowledge in DevOps, observability, event-driven programming, efficient data processing at scale, and other related areas are required for microservices deployment.

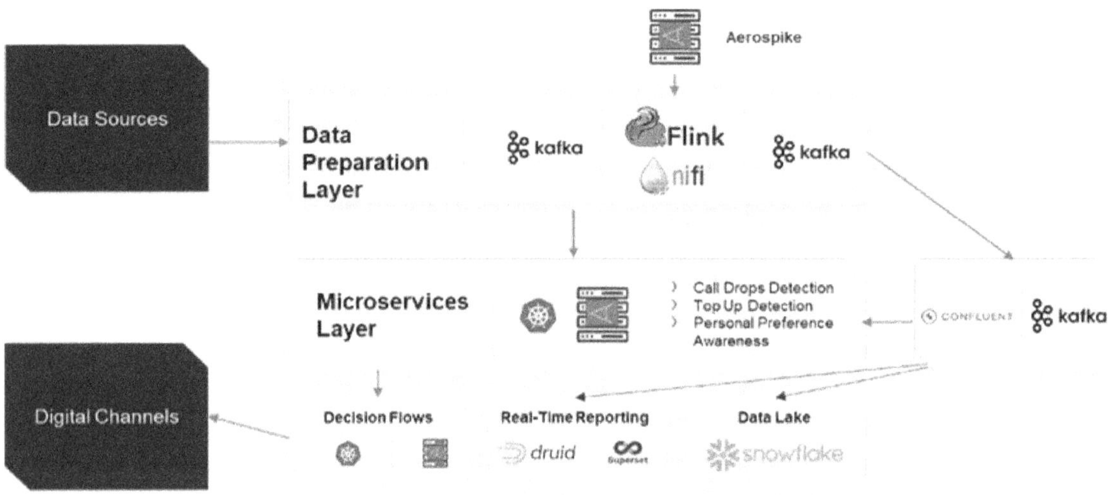

Figure 2.1: Microservices Flow diagram

Source: (Mazumder, 2022)

The data preparation layer receives input from several data sources, such as digital footprint information, service assurance parameters, and network interfaces, among others, according to the architecture's overall flow. Data intake and cleansing are handled via a nifi/flink layer within the data preparation layer, which also includes numerous on-premises and cloud kafka levels. The microservices layer receives that pristine message.

This is where things like real-time prize disbursements, call drop detection, and top-ups happen. In the subsequent steps, a multitude of outcomes are possible. In accordance with the telco's specifications, the output can be directed to a data lake or used by real-time reporting and decision layers to prompt subsequent actions. Thereafter, the chosen digital channel(s) are used to disseminate those acts.

The capacity to process massive amounts of transactions quickly and efficiently is, as indicated before, the data platform's strong suit.

2.2.1 How to adopt microservices in telecoms

Globalization is forcing telecoms to seek scalable solutions with the ability to manage millions of requests and transactions. They need to continuously adding new businesses and operations to their operations in order to expand their products. Their goal is to optimize operations, reduce fraud, and conduct preventative maintenance using big data analytics. In order to make all of the above a reality, they are embracing the use of microservices in communications.

Microservices architecture is founded on the idea that big IT systems should be divided up into smaller, easier-to-manage components that can individually accomplish tasks. Because of this, a microservices application is easier to comprehend, grow, and administer than a monolithic system. A stone can be moved easily compared to a rock. This is the same with microservices. The major advantages of the microservices architecture in telecoms include:

The telecommunications can now simply transition to microservices as the Linux Foundation is actively promoting their usage in the telecom business. To mention only two, these are Cloud Native Computing and the Open Container Initiative. Amazon, AT&T, Cisco, Google, Oracle, Verizon, and VMware are the members of these alliances—help make cloud-native computing a reality by easing the shift to microservices architectures based on containers.

Business Support Systems (BSS), Operations Support Systems (OSS), and network management are the three key areas where telecoms use microservices implementation. The three main components of BSS are telecommunications billing, customer relationship management, and order capture. Order management, inventory management, and network operations are all under the purview of OSS. Software-Defined Networks (SDNs) and Network Function Virtualization (NFVs) are two examples of modern network solutions that telecoms can use to become more agile, faster, and more scalable. They are known to be two of the most important technology enablers in the implementation of the 5G networks. The two important cloud-centric technologies currently in the market are SDN and NFV. They made it possible for telecommunications to ditch costly proprietary gear in favour of open-source software running on COTS (Commercial Off-the-Shelf) hardware, which is much more cost-effective. According to research by Global Market Insights, Inc., the NFV market is expected to surpass $70 billion by 2024. With SDN Market share being projected to exceed more than 88B by the year 2024.

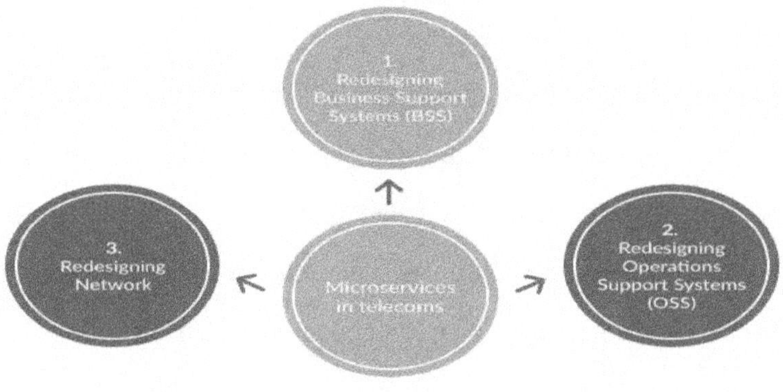

Figure 2.2: Microservices in telecom

Source: (Dziuma & Dyyak, 2020)

2.2.2 Key Components of a Microservices Framework

Telecom companies use the following key elements to run the microservices efficiently:

- **Containers:** Containers such as Docker package service as a deployment unit.
- **APIs:** Support the service-to-service communication.
- **Service Registry:** Follows and identifies micro services.

Agility in Telecommunication: The Importance of Agility Difficulties in Telecom industry cannot resist the change as the customer expectation and technological improvement are changing. In this, however, numerous obstacles discourage the telecommunication firms to keep pace with innovation. The challenge of maintaining old infrastructure and sophisticated systems, developing smooth connectivity, and data services to meet the growing demand is a grave challenge to the telecom operators.

The challenges are increased by regulatory pressure and the increased operational costs, not omitting the competitive pressure. Being aware of these trends, current concerns and even give rise to new ones helps telecom providers to be flexible, innovative and be able to keep on providing reliable and scalable services in a highly dynamic environment.

- **Complex Systems:** It is more expensive to manage complex interdependent systems and innovation decelerates.
- **Legacy Infrastructure:** It places restrictions on scalability and compatibility with new applications.
- Long Time-to-Market Monolithic architectures postpone the provision of new services and features.
- **Service Downtime:** A monolithic system, failure of one system affects all the systems, hence it is in outage state.
- **Complexity in Scaling:** These traditional systems require assistance to scale the individual aspects of the overall system, which is tedious.

Microservices have addressed such problems through offering minimal, scaled and fault-tolerant framework. This in effect will enhance operational effectiveness and increases accuracy of work.

Agile as a Business Nativity

Agility is also not merely a buzzword applied in the telecom sector, but a business requisite. The customers require expedited updates, and streamlined experiences, as well as customized solutions. To telecom providers, it entails:

- Quickening deployment cycles.
- Flexibility in keeping up with changes in the market.
- Increasing customer satisfaction by means of personalization.

MSA as a Driver for Agility

Microservice enables telecom firms to:

- Introduce new services or features fast.
- Test the new solutions without the complete redesign of systems.
- Auto-scaling manages resources in the dynamism of demands.

2.2.3 Challenges of Implementing Microservices Architecture in Telecom BSS

There are a lot of things to think about while implementing microservices architecture in the telecom BSS area. Network orchestration is one of the most important issues. The more microservices both the number and the complexity of communication among the microservices increases. A strong network orchestration mechanism is necessary to ensure that every service will work in concert and achieve maximum efficiency. This includes creating and deploying a stable system that has the ability to manage orchestration and routing of network traffic amongst microservices. Moreover, a distributed microservices network makes it more difficult to monitor and troubleshoot the network. Effective monitoring and logging should be established so that any network-related problems can be detected and solved. Generally speaking, the effective deployment of the microservices architecture of Telecom BSS relies heavily on overcoming network orchestration obstacles.

Architecture Design Principles

- **Decentralization and Independence**

The term decentralization can be applied to microservices architecture and simply means sharing the role of various services. The purpose of separating services into smaller, more manageable components called "microservices" is to improve the efficiency and flexibility of each service while also fostering greater autonomy. This decentralization allows the teams to be engaged in various services working at the same time, leading to shorter development cycles and higher productivity. Also, it enables the services to be scaled and updated more easily without any impact on the whole system. Telecom BSS systems can be more flexible and agile by disaggregating the monolithic architecture into smaller and independent services.

- **Service-Oriented Architecture**

A key part of implementing microservices design in the Telecom BSS domain is Service-Oriented design (SOA). Service-oriented architecture (SOA) enables the decomposition of large telecom systems into more manageable components that can be developed, implemented, and scaled independently. Such a decentralized style is much more modular, reusable, and flexible in the telecom sector. SOA principles can enable telecom companies to have a more flexible and efficient system architecture that is capable of responding to the highly evolving needs of Telecom Industry Revolution.

- **Scalability and Flexibility**

Microservices design has many benefits in the telecom BSS industry, including scalability and flexibility. Telecom operators can more efficiently allocate resources by decomposing large systems into smaller, independent services. This allows individual components to scale up or down depending on demand. Furthermore, telecom operators are able to swiftly modify and incorporate new features or functionalities into the system because to the modular nature of microservices. While microservices architecture has many advantages, there are unique operational hurdles when applying it to the telecom BSS domain.

- **Containerization and Orchestration**

Containerization and orchestration are the two primary components of microservices architecture that are used in the telecom BSS industry. Small, independently operated containers, or "containers," allow for the efficient delivery and operation of microservices. The flexibility of transferring containers to different settings enables easy scaling and portability. Orchestration, conversely, offers the tool of automating the process of deploying, scaling and managing containers. It will make sure that the correct containers are implemented at the correct hosts, will control the lifecycle of containers, and allow the communication between microservices to be made simple. Using containerization and orchestration, telecom BSS providers can discover an architecture that is both extremely scalable and versatile, able to endure market changes like the integration of new technologies like the Internet of Things (IoT).

- **Storage Discovery entrance and API Gateway**

Focusing on real-world difficulties and pain points in operational software stacks will allow us to create a product that is tailored to the specific demands of telecom operators and SaaS enterprises. The founders of METAVSHN set out to remedy the most pressing problems with the operational software stack management that telecom operators and SaaS companies encounter. Through watching the challenges such businesses undergo as a result of not having an integrated and seamless platform where multiple aspects of operations combine.

- **Monitoring and Logging**

The reliability and performance of Telecom BSS can be managed in part by monitoring and logging in its microservice architecture. To gain valuable insights into the system's and individual microservices' behaviour, we need monitoring and logging tools that work. As a result, we are able to improve the customer portal experience while decreasing downtime and find and fix issues earlier. Monitoring enables us to measure key measurements of response time, error rate and resource utilization whereas logging enables us to store a detailed record of each request, response, and system event. The combined result of these techniques will be to strengthen the microservices-based telecom BSS architecture and to actively debug any issues that may arise.

2.2.4 Where True Microservices Are Emerging in Telecom

Despite the challenges, certain telecom domains are moving toward **authentic microservices adoption**:

- **5G Core Networks**: The 5G Service-Based Architecture (SBA) aligns with microservices principles and supports modular network functions.
- **Customer Portals and Mobile Apps**: Front-end services are increasingly built on microservices for faster updates and user personalization.
- **DevOps Toolchains**: Adoption of cloud-native CI/CD pipelines and container orchestration platforms (like Kubernetes) is growing.

But without similar evolution in **backend systems** like billing, CRM, order management, and provisioning, **the microservices model remains incomplete.**

The Danger of Getting It Half Right

The consequences of microservices washing can be severe:

- **False confidence**: Organizations may believe they are agile and scalable when they are not.
- **Increased technical debt**: Wrapping monoliths in modern tooling adds complexity without benefits.
- **Blocked innovation**: The tight coupling remains, hindering rapid experimentation and rollout.
- **High operational cost**: Overhead increases with no real gain in efficiency or resilience.

How to Tell the Difference

It's not always obvious whether an application is truly microservices-based or simply wearing the label. Here's how to distinguish between the two:

- **Service Autonomy**: In a true microservices architecture, each service can be built, deployed, and scaled independently. In contrast, microservices washing often involves services that are tightly coupled internally and cannot function or be deployed on their own.

- **Data Ownership**: Authentic microservices own their data—each service manages its own database. If services share a common centralized database, they are not truly autonomous and remain tightly coupled.
- **Scalability**: Microservices should scale independently based on demand. In a washed architecture, the entire stack often needs to scale together, defeating the purpose of modularity.
- **Fault Isolation**: A hallmark of microservices is that the failure of one service doesn't bring down the whole system. In pseudo-microservices, a failure in one part often has cascading effects.
- **Deployment Strategy**: True microservices rely on automated CI/CD pipelines for each service, enabling rapid and isolated updates. Washed systems typically involve manual deployments or bundle multiple services into a single release cycle.
- **Design Philosophy**: Real microservices are designed using domain-driven design principles, where services are built around business functions. Microservices washing often reflects a tech-first approach, where services are split based on technical layers (e.g., frontend/backend) without regard for business logic.

Understanding these distinctions is crucial for telecom leaders to assess their true position on the modernization journey—and to avoid the pitfalls of investing in surface-level transformation.

2.3 Network Function Virtualization (NFV) Frameworks

NFV refers to the substitution of hardware by VMs that integrate network appliances. The hypervisor permits networking software and features like routing and load balancing, to run on the virtual computers.

NFV does not mandate that some hardware resources, such as firewalls and routers, be inseparably linked with communication services. Because of this delineation, network operations can dynamically provide new services without requiring the installation of additional hardware. Using network functions virtualization, implementing network components takes hours instead of months, as was the case with traditional networking. Moreover, the virtualized services are also able to run on cheaper, non-proprietary servers.

Other possibilities of using network functions virtualization are:

- **Pay-as-you-go:** Pay-as-you-go NFV models have the potential to become less expensive since the businesses pay that which is necessary.
- **Reduced appliances:** Since NFV can execute on virtual on top of physical machines, appliances are reduced and the cost of operation is lower.
- **Scalability:** Virtual machines are faster and easier to scale the network architecture, as well as, they do not need an additional hardware purchase.

2.3.1 Risks of Network Functions Virtualization

NFV improves a network's responsiveness, flexibility, and scalability. Both the time to market and the cost of equipment can be drastically decreased with its help. On the other hand, telecoms operators have been slow to embrace network operations virtualization due to security concerns. Service providers should be aware of the following hazards before deploying network functions virtualization:

- **Physical security controls are not effective**: Virtualized network components are more vulnerable to new kinds of attacks than physical hardware that is kept in a data center.
- **Malware is difficult to isolate and contain**: Virtual components that share a single virtual machine make it easier for malware to spread than physically separated hardware components.
- **Network traffic is less transparent**: Network function virtualization (NFV) necessitates more granular security solutions since traditional traffic monitoring tools struggle to detect suspicious east-west network activity.
- **Complex layers require multiple forms of security**: Blanket security policies struggle to keep network functions virtualization settings safe due to their inherent complexity and various layers.

2.3.2 Test dimensions in NFV automated testing

NFV automated testing should support the following test dimensions for baseline, security and assurance so that basic goals of solution validation, interoperability, verification of service layer agreement (SLA)/assurance, and deployment readiness can be validated.

Test dimensions for VNF:

- **Basic validation –** Verification of core services, lifecycle management (LCM) operations, and onboarding.
- **Functionality –** Verification of basic functionality, after reboot, behaviour with virtual infrastructure management (VIM) network fault, behaviour when VIM controller is restarted, VIM network restarted, and support for IPv6-Only (test by turning off IPv4 on the interfaces).
- **Performance –** Verification based on different resource configurations, max throughput, instance creation/deletion time, forwarding performance benchmarking using different traffic types, packet/frame size, and load tests.
- **Scale –** verification of multiple instances of VNF, max number of VNF, and scale-out/in.
- **VNFM interactions –** Verification of integrity of VNFD/NSD, instantiation, placement, destruction, resilience/recovery, monitoring, backup/restore, updates/roll-back, LCM after rebooting the VNF, and VNF config injection/reconfig time.
- **NFVO interactions –** Verification of VNF deployment using available network services descriptors (NSDs), live migration, and fault management and logging.

Test dimensions for NFVI:

- NFVI stack installation.
- Fault management and log collection.
- MTU changes.
- Platform awareness.
- NFVI under loaded conditions.
- Support for IPv6-only (test by turning off IPv4 on the interfaces).
- Support for service chain.

Test dimensions for MANO:

Lifecycle management – verification of VNFD/VNF image onboarding, deployment using supported flavour, and instantiation/destruction/resilience/recovery/monitoring/updates/rollbacks.

- Various VIM infrastructure.
- VNF placement/scaling.
- NFVO fault management and log collection.

- Different types of NFVO (component testing of VNFM).
- End-to-end service orchestration.
- Different types of VNFM (component testing of NFVO).
- Different types of VIM (component testing of NFVO).
- Network service instantiation.

Broad test dimensions to cover interoperability, compatibility, assurance, service orchestration, and deployment readiness:

- VNF onboarding.
- VNF config upgrades.
- Data plane performance.
- Fault and healing.
- Functionality.
- Service instantiation.
- NFV service configuration.
- Control plane scaling.
- Placement constraints.
- Use-case specific test cases.

2.3.3 Applications of NFV

NFV technology can be used for different types of packet processing in both fixed and mobile networks. This helps us understand the NFV structure better. Many real-world solutions make use of this technology, some of which include:

- **Software** – developed deep packet inspection (DPI), which allows for multidimensional reporting, easier approaches to resource application, testing, updating, and scaling in response to changing workloads, as well as advanced traffic and packet content analysis.
- **Functions** – Carrier Grade Network Address Translation, which enables clients to share a single, public IP address, and a Broadband Remote Access Server, a specialized server that makes it easier for different Internet traffic flows, including digital subscriber line (DSL), Ethernet, cable, and wireless, to converge.

- **Virtualization** – Content delivery networks (CDN) make it simpler to scale and grow content delivery services and allow additional service delivery apps to be installed on hardware.

ETSI NFV Framework 11

- **Virtualization of mobile network core** – permits more adaptable network management and establishes circumstances that make it possible to serve more traffic while making better use of resources (such as hardware consolidation, energy saving, multi-tenancy access support, which allows a single software instance and its infrastructure to serve more users, and speedier setup of new services).
- **Coordinated implementation of cloud technologies in organizations** – permits network resources and on-demand services to satisfy business needs (multiple service versions often coexist on the same hardware).

2.3.4 Advantages of applying NFV Concept

The NFV concept application aims to address several problems that prevent new and more sophisticated services from being implemented in computer networks. The virtualization of network functions, which modifies the network's architecture, infrastructure configuration, individual network units, and management style, has a significant influence on the adoption of a new work paradigm in the network environment.

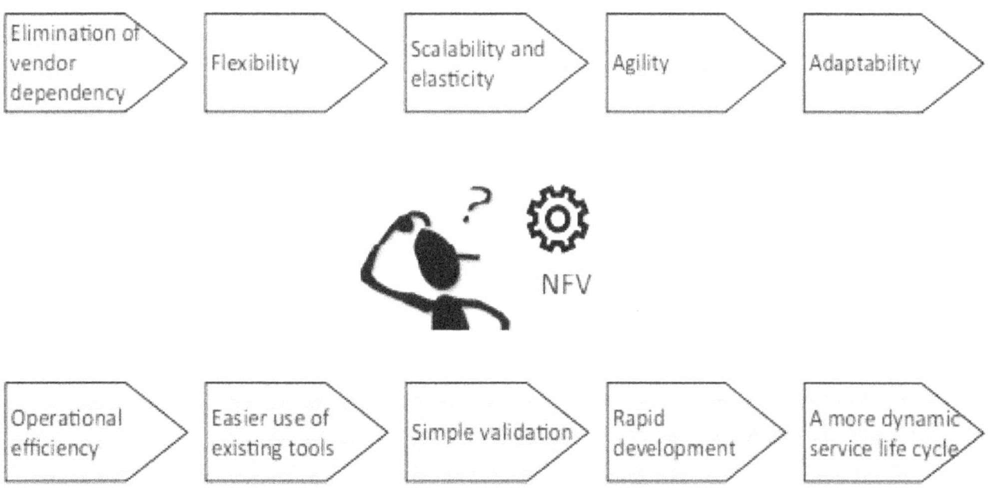

Figure 2.3: Benefits of applying NFV Concepts

Source: (Self-Created)

Those advantages primarily refer to the following:

- **Elimination of vendor dependency (no vendor lock-in)** – permits the establishment of circumstances that will enable the replacement of current equipment or the expansion of the infrastructure more quickly and affordably (equipment may be selected according to function availability, software licensing costs, and post-implementation support models).
- **Flexibility** – The ability to construct the no-cost hardware option (the NFV concept enables the use of COTS hardware) makes it possible to create a network environment that best suits service demands, run VNFs across several servers, and relocate them as needed.
- **Scalability and elasticity** – increasing the network's degree of programmability, which will enable the creation of a scalable and adaptable network environment as well as the dynamic allocation and release of resources (when necessary; this is the so-called "fast elasticity," which is mostly found in cloud environments).
- **Agility** – allows for quick network service development and deployment, cutting time to market and boosting competitiveness.
- **Adaptability** – Allows for flexibility and customization of NFV components in response to shifting client demands and other circumstances.
- **Operational efficiency** – Quick execution of network functions and services upon request, as well as the ability to apply a virtual network function or services in many network locations without requiring significant configuration modifications. Additionally, because VNF instances no longer require specialized, purpose-built hardware, running them on common hardware lowers operating expenses.
- **Easier use of existing tools** – provide it simple to use the existing tools from traditional computer networks so that they may be used even more easily in modern computer networks (on the same physical infrastructure).

2.4 Cloud Infrastructure for Scalable Provisioning

The cloud computing scalability is the ability of cloud-hosted systems to adjust their capacity in response to changing needs. The advantages of scalability to the cloud are ease, adaptability, financial savings, and improved catastrophe recovery. That is, with a scalable solution, there is no overprovisioning, and cost savings are made when the load is smaller than normal, ensuring that the solution scales itself accordingly to accept more traffic.

Scalability and its definition and significance.

Scalability Cloud computing is the capability of a cloud architecture to increase or decrease resources to meet the fluctuating requirements of the workload. This elasticity enables the businesses to add and delete the computing resources easily, without causing a major hardware investment or a substantial infrastructure modification. Scalability is an important feature of cloud computing, and it allows organizations to respond to changes in demand and achieve the best performance and customer satisfaction in a short period of time. Using cloud infrastructure that is scalable, businesses are able to ensure a high level of cloud responsiveness and service availability which are key in ensuring that they remain competitive in the current fast-paced digital world.

2.4.1 Benefits of Scalability in Cloud

The benefits of cloud computing's scalability have several benefits that affect companies of all sizes. The first benefit of scalability is that it enables businesses to promptly adjust to shifting needs, guaranteeing that their services and apps continue to function well and respond to traffic surges. Because users enjoy little downtime and quick reaction times, this flexibility results in optimal performance and increased customer satisfaction.

The other notable advantage of scaling in cloud computing is cost savings. By simply paying only the amount needed to ensure resources needed, companies can save on the cost of overproviding. This type of pay-as-you-go model will make sure that companies are better able to manage their budgets and distribute funds to the area of need.

Additionally, scalability allows the companies to expand at the international level and reach out to the customers in other areas without necessarily having a physical infrastructure in those areas. The cloud providers can enable this global connectivity and provide scalable solutions that may be deployed in many geographic regions which mean that users in different parts of the world can use the same solutions without any disruption in performance or availability.

To summarize, the advantages of the cloud computing scalability are the possibility to respond to the fluctuating needs very fast, the right to save money on using the efficient resources, and the ability to expand internationally, which improves client happiness and performance.

2.4.2 Types of scalabilities in cloud computing

In cloud computing, there are several methods for scaling, which is essentially changing how well resources can handle demand. There are three different kinds of scaling: diagonal, horizontal, and vertical.

- **Vertical scaling**

Scaling up or down is another term for vertical scaling. It's the simplest sort of scaling and ought to function immediately in any type of application. Without altering your code or application, it involves raising the allocation of instance resources (such as CPU or RAM) and guaranteeing adequate processing power. Your application's capacity to deliver content to a wider user base is essentially increased by giving instances hosting it greater resources.

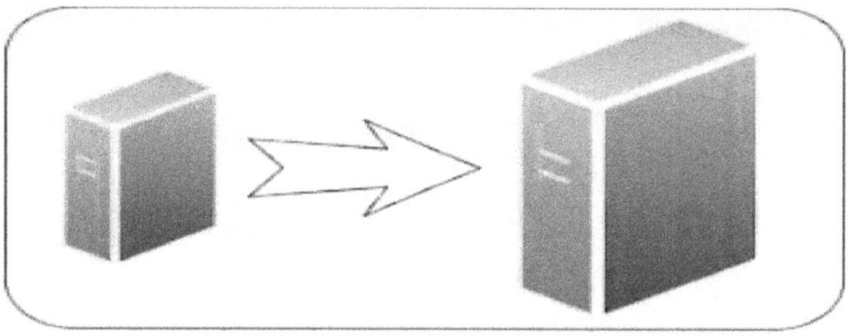

Figure 2.4: Vertical Scaling

- **Horizontal scaling**

Horizontal scaling is what you think of when you scale in or out. This one deals with expanding the number of instances operating concurrently while maintaining the same resource allocation for each instance.

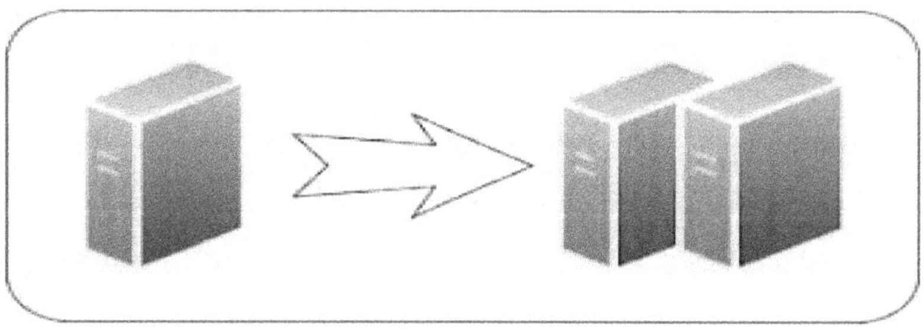

Figure 2.5: Horizontal Scaling

- **Diagonal scaling**

The diagonal scaling is a combination of vertical and horizontal scaling. You have the option to scale up your instances concurrently with scaling them out to accommodate increased traffic. A further option is to set up parameters to initiate automatic scaling in response to consumption criteria, which guarantees the best possible resource management and avoids performance deterioration.

This is helpful when a single process on a single instance starts using up the majority of its resources; in this case, the instance is scaled up, and scaling out creates smaller units to handle the remaining traffic.

2.4.3 AWS services to build scalable computing environments

Main benefits of cloud environments over on-premise environments include scalability. The cloud solutions do not require hardware, which means that businesses can scale the applications and services within a short time as compared to the long process of installing the traditional hardware. Some of the cloud-native services that are out-of-the-box and offer a high level of scalability and reliability are:

- **ASG (Auto Scaling Group)** – It is the simplest method of making your application scalable and is just a group of EC2 virtual servers. The scaling policies may be set up to scale the environment using pre-generated metrics, such as CPU or network utilization, or your own custom CloudWatch alerts. Just build a machine image (AMI) that contains your application.
- **ECS (Elastic Container Service)** – It is simpler to launch, scale, and maintain containerized applications thanks to this fully managed container orchestration service. It does all this automatically, scaling all your application containers, and the underlying infrastructure.
- **EKS (Elastic Kubernetes Service)** – This managed Kubernetes solution makes running Kubernetes on AWS and on-premises easy. It helps you establish a Kubernetes cluster as well.
- **S3 (Simple Storage Service)** – This highly accessible and expandable storage system offers several levels of storage consistency and access frequency for files. Data storage is never over-provisioned since it is implemented using a pay-as-you-go mechanism.
- **RDS (Relational Database Service)** – This managed service allows you to use the most widely used engines, such as MySQL and PostgreSQL, to deploy, maintain, and grow relational databases. Scaling up a database instance is easy and RDS also offers the feature

of dynamically scaling the amount of allocated storage as the consumed space expands. Also, it has the potential to scale out databases that have replicas of readers or writers.

- **CloudWatch** – This is an inbuilt monitoring, metrics, and logs service that provides you with the power to make your own monitored indicators alerts that can be utilized to undertake scaling activities.

2.4.4 Best Practices for Optimizing Cloud Provisioning

The following are recommended practices you may follow to get the most out of your cloud provisioning process:

1. Employ Infrastructure as code (IaC)

The concept of infrastructure as code (IaC) is an effective instrument of cloud provisioning automation. IaC tools allow defining and configuring cloud infrastructure through scripts. These versions of scripts are controllable. You can use them in the same way on a regular basis.

It is simpler to manage and maintain. The Microsoft Azure resource manager, AWS cloud, and the duplo cloud Devops automation platform are tools used to work on a multi-cloud environment. The IaC will also allow the management of cost in the clouds through avoiding configuration issues.

2. Observation and Evaluation of Performance

You are able to do this automatically and place tools to assist you in monitoring this 24/7. Measures such as the latency, throughput and error rates are monitored using tools like CloudWatch and Prometheus.

This allows you to optimize provisioning of the clouds to fit your application requirement. Unutilized resources are also discovered by means of regular monitoring. These are resources that inflate the cost of clouds without any purpose.

3. Take Advantage of Cloud-Native Security.

Incorporate traditional cloud security in cloud provisioning. Utilize tools like encryption, intrusion detection systems, and cloud-based firewalls.

By consuming cloud-native security by your cloud service provider, you can be certain that your cloud infrastructure is safe. Additionally, it complies with legal criteria.

4. Implement Continuous Integration and Continuous Deployment (CI/CD)

This incorporates upgrades on your cloud infrastructure. This approach is a guarantee of fast and secure deployment of applications. It will minimize downtime and enhance efficiency.

The Defense Information Systems Agency (DISA) (opened in a new tab) is an example of an organization that uses CI/CD pipelines in cloud-based applications. This guarantees deployment of updates in an efficient and secure way.

An example of this is the Defense Information Systems Agency (DISA)(opens in a new tab), which uses CI/CD pipelines for cloud-based applications. This ensures updates deploy efficiently and securely.

2.5 Containerization and Kubernetes Orchestration

Container orchestration can be described as Automating container deployment, maintenance, scaling, and networking over the course of their lifetime is making the deployment of software across a wide range of environments at scale.

Cloud native Application development is based on a program and its runtime environment can be packaged into a self-contained unit through the use of containers. Container orchestration is particularly relevant to those enterprises that require deploying and managing hundreds or thousands of containers and hosts. The vast majority of container orchestration applications are based on the popular open-source system Kubernetes.

2.5.1 Benefits of container orchestration

Container orchestration is associated with cost and security benefits, and development methodologies.

- **Faster development:** Containers are portable and can be run in any environment; software development opportunities are opened to faster alternatives. Container orchestration is used to create pipelines for continuous integration and continuous deployment (CI/CD), which automate software delivery across the software development lifecycle. A DevOps approach, which would shorten the time it takes to get from idea to development to execution, is closely connected to container orchestration.
- **Cost savings:** Container orchestration scales containers automatically according to your requirements and gives the necessary capacity to your applications at a reduced cost and

resource usage. Container orchestration platform has the ability to offer the flexibility required by an organization to efficiently use multiclouds and hybrid environments.

- **Security:** Containers contribute to developing software that assists teams to resolve security problems during the development phase, as opposed to requiring them to maintain or patch an application that is already deployed. This makes it possible to predict the behaviour of a container better and identify anomalous behaviour. Container orchestration also allows an organization to implement security and governance policies and divide pod policies or groups of pod policies. Container orchestration platforms also have the feature of enabling role-based access control (RBAC), which gives certain rights to users and service accounts.

2.5.2 Container orchestration tools

The container orchestration technologies offer a basis for managing the microservices and container architecture at scale. A variety of container orchestration systems are available to manage the container lifecycle. Among the well-liked choices are Apache Mesos, Docker Swarm, and Kubernetes.

Kubernetes is an open-source container orchestration technology that was first developed by developers at Google. Google donated the Kubernetes project to the Cloud Native Computing Foundation in 2015.

1. **Docker**

Docker is an open-source containerization system that builds, packages, and launches applications and their dependencies using containers.

Docker is compatible with widely used operating systems, including Linux, macOS, and Windows.

Figure 2.6: Docker

Source: (Prakash, 2022)

Docker employs Docker Swarm for orchestration and the Docker engine for containers. The host that runs an operating system for creating containers is called the Docker engine.

2. **Kubernetes**

Kubernetes is a platform for container orchestration that is open-source, also referred to as K8S. It distributes workload among containers and automates deployments. Additionally, it keeps an eye on containers and swaps out any that fail.

Figure 2.7: Kubernetes

Source: (Yalamanchili, 2019)

Initially developed by Google, Kubernetes is currently overseen by the Cloud Native Computing Foundation (CNCF).

The number of engineers utilizing Kubernetes is expanding quickly. Some companies use Kubernetes to provide orchestration services. Among them are Azure Kubernetes Services (AKS), Google Kubernetes Engine (GKE), and others.

3. **Apache Mesos**

Another orchestration tool for container-based application management is Apache Mesos. It makes use of Shipworm as a network tool and Marathon to manage clusters. It may be used for huge, intricate applications, including virtual machines, and it is fully customizable.

Figure 2.8: Apache MESOS

Source: (Yalamanchili, 2019)

This orchestration tool is managed by the Apache Mesos Project team, which has a vibrant development community.

4. **Nomad**

Designed to handle both containerized and non-containerized applications, Nomad is an open-source orchestration platform. It can operate in any cloud environment since it is cloud-agnostic.

Figure 2.9: Nomad

Source: (Freebie, 2025)

It is easy to deploy, adaptable, and seeks to remove the hassles associated with orchestration using existing technologies. Nomad's parent firm, Hashicorp, offers integrations with other products like as Consul and Vault. It may also be used with other orchestration technologies, such as Kubernetes.

2.5.3 How Kubernetes helps with container orchestration

Building application services that span several containers, scheduling containers throughout a cluster, scaling those containers, and monitoring their health over time are all made possible by Kubernetes orchestration.

Numerous manual procedures related to the deployment and Kubernetes eliminates the need for scaling containerized applications. The infrastructure offered by Kubernetes makes it easy and efficient to manage groups of hosts, which can be either physical or virtual computers running Linux containers.

In a broader sense, it facilitates the complete deployment and reliance on a container-based infrastructure in production environment. These clusters may contain hosts in public, private, or hybrid clouds. Therefore, Kubernetes is the ideal platform for hosting cloud-native applications that must grow rapidly.

Kubernetes also helps with task mobility and load balancing by allowing you to move apps without having to rebuild them.

Main components of Kubernetes:

- **Cluster:** A control plane with one or more nodes, or computers.
- **Control plane:** The set of procedures in charge of Kubernetes nodes. This serves as the foundation for all work assignments.
- **Kubelet:** This service makes sure the specified containers are launched and operating by reading the container manifests while operating on nodes.
- **Pod:** A collection of one or more containers set up on a single node. Each container within a pod shares a hostname, IP address, IPC, and other resources.

How do container orchestration tools work?

A YAML or JSON file is used to specify an application's settings when utilizing a container orchestration technology, like Kubernetes. To set up a network, locate container images, and store logs, the configuration file provides the configuration management tool with instructions.

The container management tool automatically selects the right host and plans the deployment to a cluster when a new container is deployed, taking into consideration any given requirements or limitations. The orchestration tool then manages the container's lifecycle using the settings set in the compose file.

Container-based applications and services may have their setup, lifetime, and scaling managed using Kubernetes principles. These recurrent patterns are the instruments a Kubernetes developer needs to construct whole systems.

Any container-using environment, including public or private cloud environments and on-premise servers, may employ container orchestration.

2.5.4 Types of container orchestration tools

Container orchestration systems offer tools for automating container orchestration as well as the option to install additional open-source technologies, like Prometheus, for analytics, event logging, and monitoring.

There are two primary varieties of container orchestration platforms: managed and self-managed.

- **Self-managed container orchestrators:** These systems are usually created from the ground up or make use of open-source tools like Kubernetes, give you complete control over customization. They do, however, also demand that you handle and maintain the platform, including tasks like installation, configuration, updates, and security patching.
- **Managed Kubernetes services:** Platforms like Google Kubernetes Engine (GKE) handle the difficulties involved in establishing and running the cluster infrastructure, freeing you time to concentrate on implementing and overseeing your applications. The cloud provider is in charge of overseeing setup and functionality. You may then concentrate on executing your containerized apps and only use the features.

While Kubernetes itself provides the core orchestration, a range of cluster tools work in concert that can help its security, simplify management, and enable scaling. Below is a list of related tools:

- **Monitoring and logging solutions:** Tools such as the operations suite of Google Cloud (cloud monitoring and cloud logging) are crucial for tracking the cluster's and its applications' performance and overall health.
- **CI/CD tooling:** Building container images and delivering them to the cluster may be automated with the help of systems like Cloud Build that interface with Kubernetes.

2.6 Service Lifecycle Management in Cloud-Native Environments

The configuration and upkeep of the fundamental operations, services, support components, and procedures of the cloud environment are all included in lifecycle management. Enterprises find it difficult to remain up to date with private cloud technologies due to their short release cycles. For instance, Kubernetes regularly releases fixes and security upgrades while releasing new features on a quarterly basis.

By utilizing variants of cloud systems with longer release cycles that are supported commercially, it is possible to reduce the load of regular updates on your organization.

A framework for process maturity is provided by Capability Maturity Model Integration (CMMI), which integrates people, processes, and technologies to provide capabilities. The most important CMMI process areas for lifetime management are:

- Service Continuity (SCON)
- Work Monitoring and Control (WMC)
- Work Planning (WP)
- Supplier Agreement Management (SAM)

Cloud delivery teams must use development techniques like to stay current, automated testing, continuous integration, and infrastructure-as-code. Patches and basic improvements can no longer be handled as large-scale projects.

2.6.1 Service Lifecycle Automation in Cloud

In a cloud-dominated digital world, businesses and consumers alike today want self-service, on-demand communications options together with outstanding service quality and dependability. Communications service providers (CSPs) are under extreme pressure to quickly activate services at scale and at a lower cost than ever before.

To face these issues, CSPs have been changing their operations over the last few years, and they are making good progress towards becoming Digital Service Providers (DSPs). A contemporary, simplified operations environment that removes silos and intelligently and dynamically automates the full-service lifecycle—from planning and building to fulfilment and assurance—is necessary to address these issues and become a DSP. One essential element of their digital transformation that provides a number of benefits over the current situation is the Service Lifecycle Automation (SLA) method.

On-demand services cannot be produced by CSPs using their present manual and disjointed procedures for service creation, delivery, and management. In a 5G future, such conventional processes are just too expensive, sluggish, and complicated to be viable. Although operators have made great strides in virtualizing network infrastructure and digitizing customer engagement systems, the majority of Operations Support Systems (OSS) are still highly customized and closely linked to network infrastructure domains (see Figure 10).

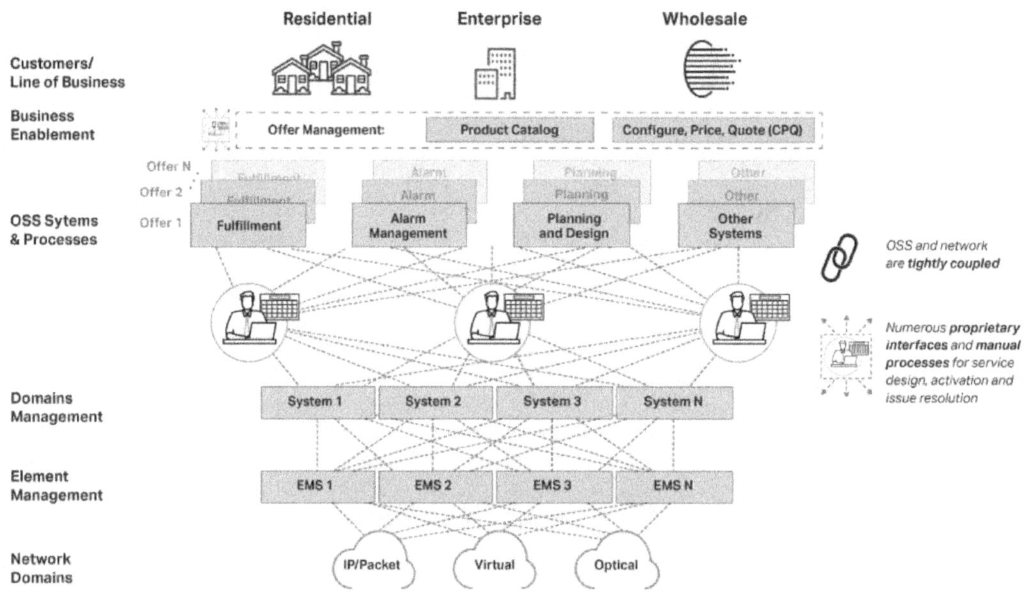

Figure 2.10: Service Lifecycle

Source: (Blueplanet, 25 C.E.)

In order to collect and correlate the data required for service design, supply, and assurance, technicians have been forced to manually visit several OSS. Because of this, launching a new service might take up to 18 months, and activating a new service order takes much longer. It is simple to understand why dynamic services cannot be supported by manual and compartmentalized techniques.

On the other hand, cloud computing systems including Microsoft Azure, Google Cloud, and Amazon Web Services are able to launch new services in a matter of hours due to automated procedures that facilitate continuous integration, testing, and delivery of new features. Nowadays, companies anticipate that CSPs will provide the same level of on-demand communications services.

2.6.2 Key Features

1. **Automated Provisioning:** Enables automatic deployment of cloud resources based on predefined templates and policies.

2. **Configuration Management:** Ensures resources are configured in accordance with organizational standards and best practices.
3. **Monitoring and Alerts:** Provides continuous monitoring of resource performance and health, with alerts for any issues or deviations.
4. **Scalability:** Supports dynamic scaling of resources to match changing workloads and demands.
5. **Policy Enforcement:** Applies policies consistently across all stages of the resource life cycle to ensure compliance.
6. **Decommissioning:** Automates the retirement of unused or obsolete resources to reduce costs and prevent resource sprawl.

2.6.3 Types of Life Cycle Management Tools

1. **Cloud Provider Native Tools:** Tools offered by cloud providers, such as AWS CloudFormation, Google Cloud Deployment Manager, and Azure Resource Manager.
2. **Third-Party Solutions:** Independent tools like Hashi Corp Terraform, Ansible, and Puppet, which provide greater flexibility and support for multi-cloud strategies.
3. **Integrated Platforms:** Comprehensive platforms like VMware Cloud Management and Red Hat Cloud Forms that offer end-to-end life cycle management capabilities.

2.6.4 Use Cases of Lifecycle Management Tools

1. **Enterprise IT Management:** Large organizations use life cycle management to ensure efficient and compliant use of cloud resources across multiple teams and departments.
2. **DevOps Automation:** Automate the provisioning and scaling of development and production environments, enabling continuous deployment and integration (CI/CD).
3. **Data Lifecycle Management:** Manages data storage resources, applying retention and deletion policies to ensure compliance and optimize costs.
4. **Disaster Recovery:** Automates the setup and maintenance of disaster recovery environments to ensure rapid recovery and business continuity in case of failures.

2.6.5 Challenges to Secure Cloud Native Applications

Security and risk experts have enormous hurdles when dealing with cloud native application:

1. **A larger number of entities to secure:** Microservices are being used by DevOps and infrastructure teams to operate their cloud-native apps by combining serverless functions,

Kubernetes, and containers. This expansion is occurring along with an ever-increasing cloud footprint. This combination increases the amount of things that need to be protected during the application lifetime and in production.

2. **Environments are constantly changing:** Today's development and DevOps teams use rapid-release cycles, which cause public and private cloud infrastructures to change often. Businesses are deploying on a weekly or even daily basis, which makes it difficult for security professionals to manage these deployments without lowering the pace of release.
3. **Architectures are diverse, spanning multi- and hybrid-cloud environments:** A diverse range of cloud services, application architectures, and public and private clouds are being used by enterprises. The whole infrastructure must be addressed by security teams, who must also consider how any holes affect security and visibility.

2.7 Chapter Summary

This chapter discussed how telecom networks are being transformed using cloud-native networks, and how monolithic systems are being replaced by microservice-based and containerized as well as orchestrated environments to provide higher levels of agility, scalability, and resiliency. It talked about the importance of the microservices in current OSS/BSS systems, their advantages in flexibility, faster time-to-market, fault isolation, as well as, efficient use of the resources, and the issues of complexity of orchestration, monitoring, security, and lifecycle management. The chapter has also discussed Network Function Virtualization (NFV) as one of the enabling factors to decouple the network functions and hardware proprietors and its frameworks, applications, benefits, risks, and extensive testing dimensions that are necessary to guarantee performance, reliability, and interoperability.

Moreover, the chapter discussed scalable cloud infrastructure and provisioning policies, such as various forms of cloud scalability, optimization best practices, and cloud-native services and automation tools. The significance of containerization and Kubernetes orchestration to telecom workloads at scale were also explained, and their advantages to cost efficiency, security and operational consistency discussed. Lastly, the chapter touched upon the topic of service lifecycle management and automation in the cloud-native, highlighting its paramount significance in facilitating the process of prompt service delivery, consistent integration, and safe functioning in 5G and beyond.

Very Short Questions

1. What architecture replaces monolithic telecom systems?
2. Name the virtualization technology for network functions.
3. Which framework tracks and manages microservices?
4. Which orchestration tool is open-source and K8S-based?
5. Term for braking systems into smaller components?
6. Name the model for process maturity in cloud?
7. What type of scaling increases instance numbers?
8. Which platform manages container deployment?
9. Which cloud service auto-scales containers?
10. Which AWS service stores scalable data objects?

Short Questions

1. Define cloud-native architecture in telecom networks.
2. List one challenge of implementing microservices in telecom.
3. What is CI/CD used for in cloud-native environments?
4. What is the role of Kubernetes in container orchestration?
5. Name two types of scaling in cloud computing.
6. What is the primary benefit of microservices in OSS/BSS?
7. Explain the main advantage of NFV over legacy hardware.
8. Give one use case of service lifecycle management.
9. What is the purpose of monitoring and logging in microservices?
10. How does cloud scalability affect cost efficiency?

MCQs (Multiple Choice Questions)

1. **Cloud-native telecom architecture primarily improves:**

   A. Cost only

   B. Agility and scalability

   C. Hardware lifespan

   D. Security exclusively

2. **Horizontal scaling refers to:**

   A. Adding CPU to instances

B. Increasing RAM of instances

C. Adding more instances

D. Reducing storage capacity

3. Service lifecycle automation reduces:

A. Time to deploy new services

B. Number of containers

C. Need for orchestration

D. Cloud scalability

4. The main function of an API in microservices is:

A. Provide storage

B. Enable service-to-service communication

C. Replace containers

D. Scale servers automatically

5. NFV enables:

A. Hardware-only solutions

B. Dynamic network service deployment

C. Manual configuration of routers

D. Fixed infrastructure scaling

6. Containers in microservices are usually managed with:

A. Apache Mesos

B. Docker

C. Kubernetes

D. All of the above

7. **Which tool is NOT a container orchestration platform?**

A. Kubernetes

B. Nomad

C. RDS

D. Docker Swarm

8. CI/CD pipelines are important for:

A. Hardware upgrades

B. Automated service deployment

C. Manual provisioning

D. Vertical scaling

9. A microservices framework typically includes:

A. Containers, APIs, Service Registry

B. Monolithic modules, ERP, Database

C. Hardware routers, Switches, Firewalls

D. Vertical scaling, Backup, VM templates

10. The NFV pay-as-you-go model primarily benefits:

A. Cost efficiency

B. Security

C. Legacy hardware integration

D. SLA violations

MCQs Answer sheet

Q1	Q2	Q3	Q4	Q5	Q6	Q7	Q8	Q9	Q10
B	C	A	B	B	D	C	B	A	A

Chapter 3: AI-Driven Telecom Provisioning and Automation

3.1 Chapter Introduction

Switching over from traditional methods to AI-based telecom provisioning and automation, the transformation goes through the stages of intelligent, self-governing networks, and ultimately responsive processes. This shift is unavoidable if the defining characteristics of modern technologies in terms of size and complexity, including 5G, the Internet of Things (IoT), and cloud-native architectures, are to be effectively managed. The ultimate goal is to create autonomous systems that can deliver the service at a higher rate, with a higher quality, and at a reduced cost of operation, thus having a very positive impact on the customer experience.

Telecom Provisioning and Automation, the telecom service provision took all the steps, which were often setting up, activating, and selling services like phone lines, internet connections, and bandwidth to users. It was a long, labor-intensive, and mistake-rich manual operation. Operations Support Systems (OSS) and Business Support Systems (BSS) were to a great extent shut off from each other, requiring a multitude of human actions to move data and orders between the systems.

3.2 Intelligent Resource Allocation and Optimization

The wise resource allocation is the smart and strategic application of data analytics, AI, and process improvement to the efficient distribution of workforce, tools, and operational resources. It aims to achieve the highest productivity, to reduce waste, and to make sure that each resource is used in accordance with the organization's objectives. Contrary to the usual allocation methods that depend heavily on manual planning and past experiences, intelligent resource allocation takes advantage of the modern technology of real-time data, predictive models, and automation to make decisions that are proactive and well-informed.

Streamlining GPU Resources using AI Task Queues is also the foremost in the currently fast-changing environment of the generative AI especially in the intensive applications such as video generation. A complex AI model requires significant computing capabilities, which, as they get more sophisticated, is considered a luxury in resource management, but not a luxury. According to industry projections, the AI hardware market is expected to hit $100 billion in 2027, which is why the role of the GPUs cannot be underestimated, and sophisticated optimization strategies are essential. The chapter discusses the complexities of the use of AI task queues to simplify the use of GPUs, boost processing times, and lower the operational platform expenses.

3.2.1 Hardware Resource Optimization: GPUs, CPUs, Memory, and Storage in Telecom

Modern telecom network optimization of hardware resources goes beyond GPUs and CPUs to cover memory and storage which is an essential element to support high-performance, AI-driven processes. Network analytics, prediction of traffic, and the provisioning of networks and networks in real-time produce large amounts of data, which need to be processed, stored, and retrieved with minimum latency. To avoid the bottlenecks of the performance, it is critical to optimize memory bandwidth and storage I/O, particularly in cloud-native and virtualized telecoms environments. Smartly controlling the GPUs, CPUs, storage and memory as a single resource pool can allow telecom operators to scale better, lower operational expenses and support applications with low latency requirements like 5G network slicing, AI-RAN, and closed-loop automation.

- **Elastic GPU Services (EGS):** Dynamic GPU Allocation the EGS enables telecommunication operators to scale their gpu on demand and address spikes in traffic without carrying the costly over-provisioned resources.
- **Tight CPU Scheduling:** Smarts workload scheduling can make sure that the CPUs are left to process the control-plane functionality, orchestration, and preprocessing workloads and offload the compute-intensive tasks to GPUs.
- **Memory Bandwidth Optimization:** The memory allocation process is made faster and smarter with intelligent caching to minimize the latency of the data access, which can be used to process real-time network telemetry and AI inference tasks at a faster rate.
- **NUMA-Aware Memory Management:** Memory locality can be optimized in multi-socket systems to support the performance of latency sensitive telecom applications by reducing the cross-node memory access time.
- **High-Performance Storage:** Utilization NVMe and SSD-based storage systems can be used to support fast read/write operations needed to store large amounts of network log data, AI training data, and historical traffic data.
- **Tiered Storage Architecture:** The smart use of tiering between hot and warm and cold storage makes sure that high-accessibility network information is easily accessible and at the same time storage cost is optimized.

- **Integrated Resource Orchestration:** Co-ordinated GPU, CPU, memory, and storage resources can be used to provide automated scaling, enhanced fault tolerance and to effectively utilize across virtualized telecom structures.

3.2.2 Importance of telecom network optimization

Network optimization in the telecom industry ensures efficient and high-quality communication services.

- **Reduces network congestion:** Telecom network optimization controls data traffic which leads to decreased network congestion. The system maintains its highest performance level during times of maximum user activity.
- **Improved service quality:** Network optimization improves service quality through its ability to transmit data with both efficiency and reliability. The system achieves better user experience because it maintains transmission operations with minimal interruptions and delays.
- **Cost reduction:** The process of optimizing a telecommunication network helps to find and correct all system points that operate with reduced efficiency. The solution will lower operational expenses because it specifically targets two major cost components which are energy usage and maintenance work.
- **Enhanced performance:** Telecom network optimization allows users to be able to manage the available resources in order to attain optimal system performance. The process requires a better bandwidth allocation that will enable better network resource utilization and reduced network traffic issues.
- **Risk management:** Network optimization helps the Telecom companies to identify the potential operational disruptions that can impact their network systems. The system allows a situation to be responded to immediately and thus prevents any possible system downtime.

3.2.3 Smart Network Optimization

The future-thinking telecom companies set up smart network optimization as their primary infrastructure strategy since it forms their primary requirement of operations. The blistering pace of digital technologies development along with the growing consumer needs demand networks to acquire greater degrees of intelligent work and scalability and instant reaction to the operations.

1. **Maximizing Operational Efficiency:** Telecom companies have problems with managing their large network systems due to the fact that the traditional process will force them to manage their whole network activities manually. This outdated system leads to the high cost of running the organization and the reduction in speed of resolving problems as well as the occurrence of unused resources. The situation can be changed with smart network optimization that involves the realization of intelligent automation technology that serves as the central element of the network management procedures.
2. **Scaling Infrastructure Seamlessly:** Telecom networks are experiencing rising network loads that are also exponentially growing as the 5G technology and the Internet of Things devices and uses of remote services expand. The providers must be able to rapidly and efficiently scale infrastructure in response to a burst in bandwidth and latency demands. The growth of intelligent network optimization helps the business to realize network expansion via its sophisticated AI-driven scalability systems.
3. **Improving Customer Experience:** The customers of telecom today want a digital experience that will operate on a 24-hour basis with no disconnections. Service providers should be able to provide their services without delays and at the highest speed without any service failures. Smart optimization will fully serve this requirement because it will give full visibility of the network that will help to adjust performance quickly.
4. **Proactive Network Intelligence:** Telecom networks operate reactive since the design of the system can only allow them to respond to problems after resolving them or when being complained by customers. With the appearance of smart network optimization technology, the current approaches to network optimization are altered. Predictive analytics with machine learning and anomaly detection systems can help the telecom companies to detect future issues in the network.

3.2.4 Challenges in telecom network optimization

- **Network complexity:** The tough situation of technological intricacies causes difficulty for telecommunications networks to be optimized.
- **Data overflow:** The massive, blazing, and diverse amount of data generated by the telecom networks make optimization efforts even more difficult.
- **Real-time optimization:** Organizations need continuous oversight of their operations because they require constant adjustments of their activities to maintain service excellence,

which needs advanced technological systems together with high-cost solutions. Organizations need to observe their operational activities in real time while they perform system updates to sustain service excellence.

- **Security risks:** The process of network optimization would create greater security dangers for the system. The process of network optimization creates an unbreakable link between the system and its security vulnerabilities.

3.3 Artificial Intelligence Techniques for Network Management

The network management systems founded on the Artificial Intelligence (AI) technology form the base of their operations and therefore, rely on it to monitor and control the network performance in an automated manner. Its method promotes the quality of decision-making and operational effectiveness based on the use of machine learning and data analytics and automated systems. The key aspects of AI-based network management are the following aspects.

- **Automated Monitoring:** The network performance is always monitored aggressively, and issues are detected instantly.
- **Predictive Analytics**: It is the ability to predict potential problems in a network, prior to their occurrence.
- **Self-Healing Capabilities:** The minimum down-time requires the repair of any defects automatically by the spring and without intervention on the part of the user.
- **Enhanced Security:** AI systems, consequently, respond to the recent security attacks much agilely and then provide quick fixes for unforeseen security incidents.

The implementation of AI-based network management systems provides organizations with three main benefits which include reduced operational expenses and enhanced customer satisfaction and increased network reliability. The innovations in the networks will put the companies in a position to respond faster and better, thus obtaining uninterrupted connection for the users. The Strategic Importance in Digital Enterprises.

In today's world where the advances in technology are very fast and continuous, the digital enterprises are extremely important. Through technology, they are able to perform their operations more efficiently, serve their customers better, and even come up with new ideas. The importance of digital enterprises is further illustrated by the following points:

- **Competitive Advantage:** Digital firms rely on novel technologies to come out the victorious side of the battle. Digital approaches have the potential to enhance operational efficiency and minimize costs as well as empower organizations to quickly react to the market trends. By implementing AI and blockchain, Rapid Innovation is not only assisting its customers in optimizing their business process but also in the creation of new value services where it also offers digital enterprise architecture as one of its solutions.
- **Enhanced Decision-Making:** Making informed decisions is the process that needs to be performed with the help of data-based insights as the main information. Digital enterprises apply big data analytics to gain a better insight into their customers and to look into market trends and to assess its operational practices that helps them identify the successful strategies.
- **Customer Engagement:** Digital platforms allow companies to communicate with their customers instantly. With the aid of social media, mobile applications, and customized marketing, businesses can rely on the power of trust and fidelity with their customers. Rapid Innovation accelerates the process of developing AI-powered tools for client engagement which are able to customize interactions and hence get the satisfaction level raised, all supported by digital enterprise services.
- **Operational Efficiency:** The implementation of automation and digital workflows has reduced the number of manual tasks, which in return has increased productivity. Digitally advanced companies are capable of enhancing their supply chains, making the best use of their resources, and thereby reducing the possibility of errors.
- **Innovation and Agility:** The innovation is driven by the digital environment. Companies have the opportunity to implement, test, and sell new ideas and products very quickly, thus being able to make adjustments according to the new consumer preferences and tech changes. Rapid Innovation provides the customers with the power to use the AI and blockchain technologies for quick and safe innovations, so they could gradually become the leader in the market; besides, tech transformation is done smoothly in case of large companies.
- **Global Reach:** Digital enterprises can work internationally, thereby attracting clients no matter where they are located. Such a move will not only create new markets but also profit points.

- **Sustainability:** A lot of digital companies are putting emphasis on sustainable methods, applying technology to minimize waste and better energy usage. Such dedication can improve the company's image and draw the attention of eco-aware customers. Rapid Innovation assists customers in the application of sustainable AI and blockchain solutions that are in line with their CSR goals.

3.3.1 Core AI Technologies

Digital companies now depend on Artificial Intelligence (AI) capabilities because AI serves as their main method for creating new products and improving their business operations. The most important AI technologies which support these organizations work through these following systems:

- **Machine Learning (ML):** ML algorithms enable systems to discover value in their data which helps them improve over time. The statement holds true for predictive analytics and recommendation systems and fraud detection among other applications.
- **Natural Language Processing (NLP):** NLP enables machines to understand and interpret human language. Chatbots, virtual assistants, and sentiment analysis make use of this technology, which leads to better customer engagement.
- **Computer Vision**: The technology being referred to is the one that enables the computer to recognize and analyze images. Some of its applications are the recognition of human faces, checking the quality of the product during the manufacturing process, and the operation of a car without a driver, among others.
- **Robotics Process Automation (RPA):** RPA, short for robotic process automation, is a tech that mechanizes human labor and thus frees up time for the staff to focus on the core activities. It is the preferred option in the sectors of finance, human resources, and customer service.
- **Deep Learning:** Deep learning, as a subset of machine learning, relies on neural networks to process and interpret large and intricate datasets. It has demonstrated high efficiency in the areas of image and voice recognition.
- **Reinforcement Learning:** The AI method being discussed is the one where the learning process is based on errors. This method has been applied to different areas, for example, self-operating robots and games played by computers.

- **Predictive Analytics:** Predictive analytics enables organizations to anticipate the future trends and actions based on the examination of the data collected from the past. This technology is of great importance in the areas of inventory management and market planning.

Digital companies need to utilize the core AI technologies for the purposes of scaling, customer satisfaction and finally, with the help of a very competitive environment, innovation. Rapid Innovation and its customers will always be partners in the technological grant through which the latter will obtain the business objectives quickly and efficiently.

Refer to Figure 1. It is a visual representation of the strategic importance that the digital businesses and the building blocks have in the economy.

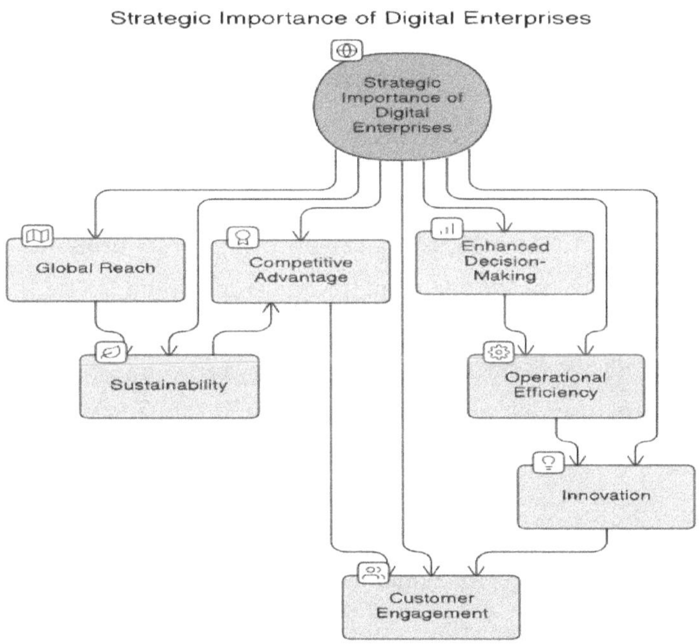

Figure 3.1: Strategic Importance of Digital Enterprise

Source: (Anglen, 2025)

3.3.2 Best Practices for Integrating AI in Network Management

AI application to network management is a case of extremely radical transformation, still, the project's triumph will be predominantly decided by the implementation. Adhering to the best practices will lead to a much better and smoother process of implementation and higher-quality results.

- **Strategic Planning:** Assess your specific needs before the introduction of an AI system in your organization. Locate the areas where the most impact can be made by AI, such as minimizing downtime and enhancing security. Make sure that AI projects are in line with business goals so that they can be credited with giving measurable value. A well-defined plan from the get-go will allow you to prevent unnecessary expenses and concentrate on obtaining significant outcomes.
- **Selecting the Right Tools:** It is very important to choose the right AI tools. Assess the solutions considering scalability, integration with your current systems and support for your team. Search for tools that are specifically created for network management, for example, those that provide predictive analytics or real-time monitoring. Examine the software's capabilities and choose it wisely as your business will be growing and changing.
- **Training and Upskilling:** In many cases, the implementation of AI means that the current skills will not be enough. The commitment to training will make the AI tools comprehension and usage by the team members effective. The transition can be smoothened and the employees can be made more confident in the use of the technology through workshops, certifications, or hands-on training sessions. By upskilling, you can prevent the building of resistance to change while at the same time ensuring that your workforce can harness the full potential of AI.
- **Continuous Monitoring:** AI systems are not "set it and forget it" solutions. Conduct a periodic performance evaluation to ascertain if they are still aligned with your goals. Utilize the feedback for algorithm adjustment, accuracy improvement, and handling any new issues. Keeping track of the performance constantly is a way to retain the effectiveness of your AI systems in the long run.

If you take advantage of best practices, your company will be able to gain the maximum from AI integration and at the same time, keep the risks at a minimum.

3.3.3 Machine Learning Models for Traffic and Demand Prediction

In order to control vehicle movement, lessen congestion, and provide the best (least time- or energy-consuming) route, traffic prediction entails estimating the volume and density of traffic flow. For two types of organizations, traffic forecast is crucial (we're not talking about people organizing a weekend trip, you know).

local and national authorities. Many cities have used intelligent transportation systems (ITS) that facilitate traffic management and urban transportation network design throughout the past ten to twenty years. By alerting users to current road conditions and modifying road infrastructure (such as lamps), these systems employ produced forecasts and current traffic data to increase transportation efficiency and safety.

Demand forecasting is the technique of estimating and projecting future consumer demand for a good or service through predictive analysis of previous data. Syntetos-Boylan Approximation (SBA), Holt's Winter Method, Croston Method, and Simple Moving Average are statistical techniques for forecasting. For intermittent forecasting, Croston and SBA are primarily utilized.

The Machine Learning approach to forecasting involves –

- Time Series Analysis
- Regression Modelling
- Deep Learning Modelling

3.3.4 Machine Learning Models for Demand Prediction

1. Data Pre-processing

It is a crucial strategy for every machine learning effort. But when it comes to time series data, it becomes more complex. To ensure that trend and seasonality are not affected, we must pre-process the data. Pre-processing can be carried out as follows:

- **Anomaly Detection & Correction** – It is the process of identifying uncommon occurrences, objects, or observations that are suspicious due to their notable deviations from typical patterns or behaviors. Finding anomalies in time-series data can be challenging since trend and seasonality must be taken into account.
- **Breakpoint Analysis** – Demand data may be analyzed using breakpoint analysis to identify changes or interruptions in demand levels. This can remove old data from the past that is no longer relevant.
- **Seasonality and Trend Calculation** – Seasonal decomposition can be used to calculate trend and seasonality. This provides insight into the general pattern and any seasonality.

2. Time Series Analysis

ARIMA is a way to perform Time Series Analysis. There are few variants of ARIMA –

- **ARIMAX** – Standard ARIMA with an additional feature to train using exogenous factors.
- **SARIMA** – Seasonal ARIMA
- **SARIMAX** – Seasonal ARIMA with exogenous factors
- **Auto ARIMA** – Automatically tries to find best fitted ARIMA considering seasonality and exogenous factors

Pros

- Accuracy is very high
- Easy to implement
- Can generate a model with few data points. In this case, a minimum of 12 data points were used to generate this model

Cons

- In a few cases, it fails to identify trends or seasonality
- In some cases, it identifies the incorrect trends and extrapolates the data exponentially

3.3.5 Machine Learning Models Used for Traffic Prediction

Numerous machine learning methods are used to predict the traffic flow, and they have their merits:

1. **Regression Models:** Linear regression and its variations are the models of the first order, which base their prediction of the volume of traffic on the trends of historical data. They are basic parts but they give a good beginning point on the study of the trends in traffic.
2. **Support Vector Machines (SVM):** The Support Vector Machines (SVMs) algorithm applies intricate boundary techniques in differentiating various traffic situations that comprise of light traffic and moderate traffic and heavy traffic. It is very effective in the patterns that exhibit non-linear trends and different forms of data.
3. **Neural Networks:** Deep learning approaches in time series forecasting show better results than conventional techniques because their RNN and LSTM systems can track traffic data through its temporal patterns. Because of this feature, the models can foretell the traffic flow with an extremely high level of accuracy, regardless of whether the period is just a few minutes or several hours.

4. **Ensemble Methods:** Models like Random Forests and Boosting often combine several different models in order to improve prediction accuracy and robustness.

Role of Data in Traffic Prediction Models

Machine learning models thrive on quality data. Cities collect data through:

- Traffic cameras and sensors
- GPS devices in vehicles
- Mobile apps and social media
- Weather stations

3.3.6 Five Factors That Influence AI Demand Forecasting Accuracy

Speaking of a real demand forecasting model, we now need to talk about the internal and external variables that may affect its performance. The machine learning (ML) model's prediction accuracy rate is unlikely to be 100% because it will base its forecasts on historical data. On the other hand, we may reduce such dangers during the actual model-building step by comprehending the following.

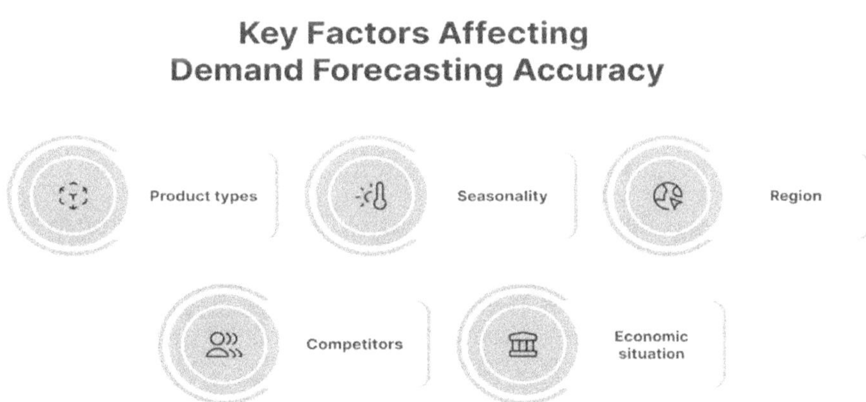

Figure 3.2: Factors Affecting Demand Forecasting Accuracy

1. **Product Types and Modeling Errors**

When choosing an ML demand forecasting model, the product type is a crucial consideration.

For instance, the forecast of selling 90 cases is better than the forecast of 110 cases for a perishable commodity with an actual demand of 100 cases. Even if the real inaccuracy is the same amount, missing 10 cases of sales is preferable to waste 10 cases.

2. **Seasonality**

The seasonality cycle is essential for forecasting demand for any product.

For instance, if you sell hiking tents, demand seems to rise seasonally during the summer, peaking in a certain month in your region. Since we require a year's worth of data at the very least to compute the seasonality, the machine learning model's prediction won't be correct if we use data for just five months to train it. A three-month data collection will be sufficient to begin training the model and generating projections for items like spoons and forks whose demand doesn't change seasonally. However, it always relies on the product itself as well as other outside variables like competition or the amount of vacations during a specific time frame.

3. **Regional Impacts on Model Performance**

Regional characteristics, such as consumer behavior and cultural influences, have a significant impact on machine learning demand prediction models:

- Depending on a customer's location, marketing strategies may be geographically customized and have distinct effects.
- Regional variations in holidays may be taken into account when modifying the model.
- Certain data may not be used in some areas due to legal concerns or regulations.

4. **External Data Richness**

If your model just relies on POS data, it will be ignorant to the real-world factors that drive demand. Promo calendars, weather variations, movement patterns, and local events are examples of external data sources that provide the algorithm with the context it needs to distinguish signal from noise. Enhancing ML forecasting models with external signals increases prediction accuracy by 10% when compared to raw data baselines, according to BCG's 2023 study on AI-driven integrated business-planning platforms.

Therefore, it is advised that your AI demand forecasting model include this data dynamically.

5. **Economic Situation**

Businesses and ML demand forecasting models are impacted by the status of the economy.

For instance, while sales of inexpensive goods may increase during economic downturns, demand for pricey goods is likely to drop. Therefore, while developing artificial intelligence models, trends and the state of the economy should be taken into account as they are not external elements.

3.4 Data-Driven Decision-Making in Telecom Operations

Data-driven decision-making (DDDM) is changing the telecommunications industry, offering it an evidence-based solution to overcome the traditional use of intuition-based decision-making. This method entails the methodical gathering, examination and understanding of tremendous volumes of data- between customer utilization trends and network results measurements and market trends as well as banking information- to direct strategic and operational decisions. Telecom operators will get a thorough, unbiased view of the complex activities within their businesses and the continuously changing terms in the market through the use of real-time data made accessible by sources like the Internet of Things (IoT) and interaction with clients. The power of relying on hard data and measurable proof, rather than on presumptions and the personal views of the highest paid person, gives telecom companies the advantage of improving the accuracy and trustworthiness of their plans, handling risks more efficiently, and having easy transitions of their projects to such business results as an increase in revenue and customer satisfaction.

3.4.1 The Benefits of Implementing Data Analytics in Telecom

With telecom converging on value-added services as their revenue stream, cloud hosting and remote management of IT operations have been on the rise just like the need for the infrastructure.

- **Predict And Prevent Network Issues:** Proactive Monitoring of Network Performance Helps Identify Potential Bottlenecks or Failures Before They Occur, Ensuring Uninterrupted Service.
- **Personalize Customer Experiences:** Understanding User Behavior Enables Telecom Companies to Tailor Services and Offers, Boosting Customer Satisfaction and Loyalty.
- **Optimize Resource Allocation:** Data Analytics Aids in Optimizing the Deployment of Resources, Whether It's Network Bandwidth or Customer Support Staff.
- **Drive Revenue Growth:** By Identifying New Market Opportunities and Understanding Customer Preferences, Telecom Companies Can Develop Targeted Campaigns and Introduce Relevant Services.

3.4.2 Benefits of Becoming a Data-Driven Telecom Enterprise

Telecom companies will increasingly use AI in their operations, and this will be the main influence throughout the company. The company will transition from its current operational methods to its previous operational methods through their new approach to service creation and customer engagement and network operations and market research activities.

1. **Real-time Adaptability:** Real-time results provided on the platform not only support the opinion on managerial course of action but may as well suggest otherwise if objective intelligence gathered to support them. They can detect the areas of concern before turning into service troubles by constantly monitoring traffic, devices, and the surroundings. The use of dynamic scaling, automated rerouting, and anomaly detection leads to less service deterioration and quicker time to repair. Such a high degree of responsiveness guarantees no break in connectivity, top-notch user satisfaction, and a network that adjusts to customer demand instantly.
2. **Greater Customer Value Creation:** Telecoms analyzing customer, device, and network data very well will not have just a personalized service but also a competitive edge. Businesses are able to foresee customers' requirements, provide offers just at the right moment, and, design communication that will be natural and related to the customer. The use of intelligence has allowed different companies to provide service and make money from each interaction point using. One of the benefits is the creation of more satisfied customers, whom usually the companies have better loyalty, and the relationships are built with accuracy and knowledge.
3. **Operational Clarity and Efficiency:** Basically, the use of data by telecoms has empowered everyone in their value chain to see far ahead and thus they have eliminated the guesswork in their processes. The operational departments are lapping up these insights already because they are getting real-time information on the health of their assets, the performance of the network, the productivity of the workforce, and the changes in the environment around them. The engineering departments can now easily tell when there is going to be a failure, which fix is going to have the most impact thus they can decide how to distribute their resources in the most effective way. Service departments are now able to provide better service with increased speed and accuracy. The overall picture painted by these new insights becomes the basis of new operational rhythms with less waste going on, faster workflows, and much better cost-to-serve model overall.
4. **Stronger Revenue Insights:** Telecommunications companies that adopt analytics gain a detailed comprehension of market changes and customer value. The use of segmentation in real-time shows the rise of new clusters with high usage, changes in the consumption of

content, and the prospects of cross-sell or upsell. The heads of the companies can spot the assets that are not fully utilized, assess how well the products are doing, and bring to the market the new services that are supported by data that are specifically designed to meet the needs of the market. This understanding allows the firm to penetrate new markets, to depend less on trial and error, and to surely maintain the rivalry in the fast-paced changing environment.

5. **Sustainable Competitive Advantage:** A telecom firm that relies heavily on data changes its strategy from simply monitoring the market to proactively foreseeing its requirements. They no longer wait for shifts in the market or for complaints to be registered; rather, they anticipate customers' needs and directly provide user-friendly, smooth and even better than expected experiences. The constant stream of insights allows them to come up with solutions quicker, provide robust services and stand out even in a market full of competitors. This benefit that lasts for a long time gets bigger over time and it molds the company to be one that is designed for quick changes, modernity and continuous leadership.

Evolving into a top telecom operator based on data analysis is mainly a transformation from managing a network to managing a smart business powered by insights - a business that creates value quickly, accurately, and with foresight.

3.4.3 Challenges in Data-Driven Decision-Making in Telecom Operations

1. **Information Islands Within Telecom Systems:** Telecom operators get data aggregated on networks, billing, customer support, and third-party tools however the data is frequently stored in separate silos. Lack of system interoperability will result in decision-makers having biased or slow information, which is the opposite of being data-driven.
2. **Bad Data Quality and Inconsistency:** Incomplete, distorted, or inconsistent data is an issue that is always present in telecom settings. In case of incorrect or un-recent input data, analytics models can give inaccurate outcomes that can result in erroneous decisions in operations and a wastage of resources.
3. **Complexity of Real Time Processing:** The operations of Telecom need almost real time decision, particularly on the optimization of the network and fault mitigation. Such technical complexity and high latency requirement would require a complex infrastructure

and most operators are yet to implement it successfully when handling large amounts of streaming data.

4. **Scalability and cost of Infrastructure:** Processing telecom data on a large scale demands cloud and analytics platforms that are scalable. Yet, installing legacy infrastructure upgrades and ensuring high-performance data pipelines may be costly, and the optimization of costs is a significant concern of the operators.
5. **Skill Gap and Shortage of Talent:** The development of advanced data analytics and AI systems involves the employment of qualified specialists around data engineering, data scientists, and ML specialists. Lots of telecom organizations are deprived of adequate expertise, which slows adoption and diminishes the data-driven strategy.
6. **Privacy and Data security issues:** Telecom data contains confidential customer and operational data. Data privacy, regulatory compliance, and resistance to cyber threats introduce additional complexity which usually limits the freedom of using data to generate analytics.
7. **Legacy Telecom Systems Integration:** Most telecom companies are still on the ancient systems that were not built to support current analytics. The incorporation of these systems with new areas of data is costly in time and is prone to errors, resulting in postponement of decision-making.

3.4.4 Top Benefits of Data-driven Decisions for Telcos

Personalized approach: Decisions based on advanced data analytics facilitate the offering of custom proposals to clients. Instead of simply looking at standard points, e.g., age, gender, and demographics, telcos have additional data resources available, such as browser history and call records. According to the numbers, firms that invest in personalization might get over 40 percent return in revenue.

Faster rollout of relevant services: Big Data helps with faster and more efficient analysis of incoming data, which allows for detecting individual patterns for customer behavior and preference analysis. Owning this information helps a company prepare new releases swiftly and with better confidence and quality. There's also no need to spend extra time and resources on advance testing or trials of the service or product. It allows faster rollout while helping to improve existing services and products.

Optimized workflow: According to Dell's Big Data stats, 85 percent of telcos point to network optimization as a top priority for the industry. The analysis of information that comes from user devices or network equipment helps detect where data flow is interrupted. Clearing the way for efficient load balancing commits to even distribution. As a result, using these insights significantly improves the dependability and effectiveness of telecom services.

Swift adoption of innovation: Receiving information from diverse sources can help companies create innovative products and services. To advance in these innovation efforts, 60 percent of organizations apply data analytics. Using those insights to guide service or product development also helps businesses improve their performance and provide the right solutions for their customers.

Competitive edge: Staying ahead of competitors plays a crucial role for telcos and data analysis plays a major role in their doing so. By drawing out requisite numbers and implementing data-driven decisions, an organization can gain a significant competitive advantage.

3.4.5 Real-World Applications of Data Analytics in Telecom

The transformative power of data analytics is evident in various real-world applications within the telecom industry:

1. **Fraud Detection and Prevention**: Advanced analytics can identify unusual patterns that indicate fraudulent activity, protecting both customers and the company's bottom line.
2. **Smart Cities and IoT**: Telecom companies leverage data analytics to support the infrastructure of smart cities, ensuring efficient communication between IoT devices.
3. **Customer Segmentation**: By categorizing customers based on usage habits, telecom operators can create more effective marketing campaigns and service plans.

For instance, Vodafone has implemented data analytics to enhance its customer segmentation efforts, leading to more targeted and successful marketing campaigns.

3.5 Closed-Loop Automation and Self-Healing Mechanisms

Closed-loop automation is an advanced model of control wherein the system keeps track of its performance and the surrounding environment and automatically modifies its behaviors due to a closed-loop feedback mechanism to operate within a desired state without human intervention, as opposed to open-loop systems that do not have a feedback system. This is the foundation of self-healing mechanisms which support systems such as IT infrastructure, telecommunication networks, and industrial control systems to autonomously detect, diagnose and recover faults or anomalies in real-time resulting in resilience and limited downtime. The fundamental cycle is a constant loop and is sometimes known as the detect, analyze, act, and learn (or MAPE - Monitor, Analyze, Plan, Execute) cycle: the system always collects a lot of telemetry data (logs, metrics, traffic patterns, etc.) at all its components; this data is processed and analyzed, usually with the help of advanced artificial intelligence (AI) and machine learning (ML) models, to establish anomalies, relationships between events, and the real root cause of an issue, not just simple alert thresholds. When a decision has been reached, the system automatically responds with a correction action, e.g., rerouting network traffic, reconfiguring system parameters, restarting a malfunctioning container within a Kubernetes cluster, or even the provisioning of a new virtual resource, all based on preset policies and confidence levels to the human operator. This is what makes this loop so close that the system checks the result of its action and recycles the results and new data into the analytics/learning step and evolves its decision models and ameliorates its future reactions, thus getting ever more intelligent and efficient with each step.

3.5.1 Closed Loop Automation

The oversight of a network's automation and management capabilities is called closed-loop automation. Closed-loop automation uses data and analytics to track and evaluate network events like failures and congestion and take appropriate action to address any problems. In order to facilitate self-optimization, the loop refers to the feedback loop of communication between tracking, identifying, modifying, and optimizing the network's performance. The solution functions as the fundamental requirement for enabling self-driving network technology. about 90 percent of network operators now treat automation as their primary operational focus which enables them to enhance their business processes and deliver faster time-to-market for their profitable services. The use of custom scripts as well as zero-touch provisioning to automate basic administrative and configuration tasks are just a few examples of how network operators envision their future. The most sophisticated among them have already started to enjoy the advantages of SDN/NFV which not only facilitate the control of services in a better way but also present the service agility aspect as a whole and practically eliminate the manual interference in important operational processes through closed-loop automation.

Where Is Closed-Loop Automation Being Used?

- **Telecom:** For automated network healing and performance optimization
- **Finance:** For fraud detection and real-time risk mitigation
- **Retail:** For dynamic pricing based on inventory and demand
- **Manufacturing:** For predictive maintenance of machinery
- **Healthcare:** For real-time patient monitoring and alerting systems

Why Should Businesses Care?

1. **Speed & Efficiency:** Previously renormalizing errors (almost) hours or days as with separation of power measurements, are fixed in minutes.
2. **Reduced Operational Costs:** With less manpower, a margin of human error is less, thereby the more semantic concentration enhances the resource utilization.
3. **Scalability:** CLA allows having more capacity to grow without necessarily expanding its workforce or expenses.
4. **Enhanced Customer Experience:** Improved Customer satisfaction will follow as fewer interruptions will be caused by issues proactively resolved.
5. **24/7 Uptime:** An insight into the interest of hibernation; the future is closed looped systems monitoring even when workstations clock out.

3.5.2 Self-Healing Mechanism

The test automation self-healing solution can fix all problems which occur when web elements change their ID Name XPath or CSS properties because these changes cause test scripts to fail. The system uses automatic methods to find and resolve issues which prevents test failures while enhancing system dependability. Self-healing test automation uses advanced artificial intelligence technology to enable automated test scripts which automatically detect and fix their own errors without requiring human help. The standard test automation system experiences test failures because of three factors which include dynamic changes to user interface elements and the element locators that fail to work and the system that operates in an unpredictable manner. Self-healing automation uses artificial intelligence and machine learning to maintain test operations while it automatically fixes broken locators and generates new test scripts which results in reduced maintenance work and enhanced testing accuracy.

3.5.3 Working on Self-Healing in Test Automation

The self-healing feature in test automation uses a systematic method to improve test execution efficiency. The self-healing test automation process consists of these main operational steps.

1. **Element Identification**: The framework identifies the location of UI elements and log the identity of elements, like ID, name, CSS selector, XPath, and text attributes. The system does total profiling that identifies items across the system even when they are subjected to change.
2. **Test Execution**: The framework attempts to locate an element through primary detection during the examination of the tests. The framework uses secondary attributes or other approaches in identifying the element in case an element is absent.
3. **Issue Detection and Analysis**: When an element is not found based on the expected identifiers, the system will evaluate the failure as well as will take into account the options of revising the UI or the structure of the application.
4. **Self-Healing Action**: The framework modifies the test script immediately after the identification of the new features or identifiers of the modified feature. Consequently, the subsequent test runs are able to locate and interact with the element automatically, without man-hand intervention.

3.5.4 How Does AI Contribute to Self-Healing Tests?

Artificial Intelligence is a major factor that makes it possible for automated tests to rejuvenate themselves. Machine learning (ML) and natural language processing (NLP) are among the AI techniques that are utilized for identifying modifications in the application and for performing test updates automatically. Listed below are the various avenues through which AI boosts self-healing tests:

- **Object Recognition and Visual Testing**: The analysis of visual factors in the application is done by AI in order to recognize the changes in the UI. It applies the image recognition technology to identify the buttons, links, and other UI objects that may have shifted their positions or appearances. This ensures that tests are successful in cases where there are visual modifications.
- **AI-Based Element Locator Prediction**: AI predicts and updates locators for UI elements whenever there is a change. Through machine learning, it is possible to spot the locators

that are the most stable, which in turn lessens the number of test failures that were caused by dynamic elements.

- **NLP and Semantic Understanding**: AI utilizes Natural Language Processing (NLP) to comprehend the text and modify the tests according to it. In case the labeling of a button gets altered, the AI interprets its significance and alters the testing process without any manual intervention.
- **Real-Time Test Monitoring and Self-Correction**: The AI expertly handles the testing process by constantly supervising the execution of tests, identifying the problems and recommending solutions. When a test doesn't pass because of a non-existent element, the AI looks for another locator or another way of interacting with it.

3.6 Chapter Summary

This chapter has been very informative about the changes that AI-based provisioning, intelligent use of resources, and auto-management of networks are bringing to the telecom industry. It clearly pointed out the evolution of the old manual systems used in telecom that were confined in different departments, making it hard for them to share information and thus being incapable of dealing with 5G, IoT and cloud-native environments, to being data-driven and autonomous systems that can even handle the mentioned complexity. The discussion mainly revolved around smart and quick resource allocation plans, AI-operated network management, and traffic and demand prediction through machine learning techniques, among other things. All these would in turn lead to the triple benefit of improved efficiency, reliability, and customer experience and at the same time reduced operational costs. The chapter brought attention to yet another aspect, which was the data-based decision-making and closed-loop automation reliance in the creation of the self-healing, adaptable telecom networks. With the integration of AI, real-time analytics, and feedback loops, telecom companies will be allowed to make adjustments to the network performance, manage the resources optimally and also instantly react to the changing needs. Despite the challenges pointed out by the chapter, such as data silos, problems with scalability and a shortage of skilled personnel, it has been concluded that embracing AI-powered automation and analytics is a must if one wants to build a strong and future telecom system that can easily gain over the rivals for a long time.

Very Short Questions

1. Type of memory management in telecom?
2. Abbreviation of Operations Support Systems?
3. AI technique for traffic prediction?
4. Technology behind self-healing networks?
5. Storage system type for AI logs?
6. Core AI for language understanding?
7. Primary goal of intelligent resource allocation?
8. Closed-loop automation cycle?
9. Model for demand prediction?
10. Resource scaled by EGS?

Short Questions

1. Name one challenge of implementing AI in telecom.
2. How does real-time monitoring improve customer experience?
3. Why is integrating legacy telecom systems difficult for AI adoption?
4. How does AI improve resource allocation in telecom?
5. How does closed-loop automation reduce downtime?
6. What role do GPUs play in AI-driven telecom networks?
7. Why is data-driven decision-making important in telecom operations?
8. Give one benefit of smart network optimization.
9. What is the function of self-healing mechanisms in test automation?
10. How does predictive analytics help network management?

MCQs (Multiple Choice Questions)

1. **Closed-loop automation cycle is also called:**
   A. MAPS
   B. MAPE
   C. RMA
   D. SLA
2. **Network optimization reduces:**
   A. Congestion

B. AI performance

C. Memory bandwidth

D. Customer engagement

3. GPUs in telecom are optimized for:

A. Low latency and AI tasks

B. Storing logs only

C. Human resource allocation

D. Billing systems

4. Time series forecasting models include:

A. ARIMA

B. SARIMA

C. Auto ARIMA

D. All of the above

5. Self-healing test automation uses:

A. Manual scripts only

B. AI and ML

C. Static locators

D. Spreadsheet monitoring

6. EGS stands for:

A. Elastic GPU Services

B. Enhanced Grid System

C. Enterprise General Storage

D. Efficient Gateway Scaling

7. Closed-loop automation primarily helps in:

A. Human error increases

B. Automatic network adjustment

C. Manual monitoring

D. Hardware failure

8. Data-driven telecom operations benefit by:

A. Guesswork in decision-making

B. Real-time adaptability

C. Increased downtime

D. Manual scaling

9. AI techniques for network management include:

A. Predictive Analytics

B. Self-Healing

C. Automated Monitoring

D. All of the above

10. Which factor affects AI demand forecasting accuracy?

A. Seasonality

B. Regional impact

C. External data richness

D. Random number generation

MCQ Answer sheet

Q1	Q2	Q3	Q4	Q5	Q6	Q7	Q8	Q9	Q10
B	A	A	D	B	A	B	B	D	A

Chapter 4: Autonomous Networks and Zero-Touch Provisioning

4.1 Chapter Introduction

This chapter 4th is about the radical world of autonomous networks and zero-touch provisioning, which are the concepts that are moving the design, deployment, and management of modern networks to a new plane of reality. The extent and sophistication of networks grow and traditional ways of configuring a network manually and reactively are failing to keep pace and this leads to inefficiency and the threat of making a mistake. The autonomous networks are based on automation, intelligent analytics, and policy-based control to offer systems in which configurations, optimization, and self-healing can be accomplished with minimal human intervention, a fundamental shift of a static to an adaptive approach to network operation.

This chapter is also an exploration of the concept of zero-touch provisioning, another key facilitator in the autonomous network capability. Zero-touch provisioning also allows the automatic deployment and configuration of devices and services when they start operating, which rules out the chance of human error in the setup and reduces the time that was spent to deploy devices. When used together with autonomous network systems, zero-touch provisioning provides consistency in policy enforcement, scalability and adherence to network infrastructures. The chapter describes the way next-generation networks may achieve operational intelligence, operation efficiency, and scale resiliency.

4.2 Concepts and Levels of Network Autonomy

Autonomous networks represent an advanced stage in network evolution, where rule-based automation is replaced by intelligent operations that adapt and execute real-time business-critical tasks autonomously.

The autonomous networks are constructed based on the following major pillars:

- Close-loop agentic automation.
- Intention-based interactivity and interoperability.
- Smart information handling.
- Open platforms and APIs

The network autonomous domains are at the very bottom that have self-x capabilities that allow domains to deploy, configure, monitor, maintain, and retire independently.

Autonomous network operations connect system components. Actionable updates in the form of network updates are generated as a result of dynamic intent management and agentic AI closed-loop automation, to make sure that high-level business goals are converted into actionable form. It includes the analysis of the intents, adaptation to the shifting conditions, and conflict resolution to coordinate and sustain the process of providing advanced services on all OSS/BSS layers, vendors, and network domains.

Autonomous networks establish a foundation for new business paradigms, enabling streamlined operations, scalable services, and faster time-to-market for advanced network offerings such as differentiated connectivity and APIs.

4.2.1 What is an Autonomous Network?

An autonomous network runs with minimal to no human intervention—able to configure, monitor, and maintain itself independently.

Automation itself, and the idea that technologies could be self-provisioning, self-diagnosing, and self-healing, has been around for some time. But with advances in Artificial Intelligence (AI) and cloud technologies, such fanciful notions are quickly becoming realities.

Nowadays, most of us use AI-enabled apps when we ask Apple's Siri or Amazon's Alexa for help with a task. And even streaming services like Netflix help us pick movies and TV shows using AI.

In the world of terrestrial and submarine networks, AI and the elements that make up the cloud are converging to enable the next level of networking.

Those elements include:

- **Virtually boundless compute resources**: Modern CPUs can be clustered to offer massive, almost unlimited parallel processing power.
- **Essentially unlimited storage**: Storing a single, massive set of data across multiple processing platforms—within the same data center or across numerous physically separated data centers—is not only feasible, it's now common.

- **Dynamic connections**: Agile, on-demand bandwidth—provisioned with the precise connection needed depending on the type of data in transit—is a critical component of an autonomous network.
- **Open-source software**: Open-source solutions like Hadoop are at the center of AI transforming networks.
- **Big data**: For an autonomous network, the gathering and analysis of data from network sensors leads to better detection of patterns and anomalies.
- **Sensors**: Embedded sensors, and the data they produce, form the foundation of an autonomous network infrastructure

4.2.2 Benefits of Autonomous Networks

Autonomous networks shift operations and maintenance away from static rule-based automation – managed by humans, towards more dynamic intent-based automation – governed by humans. In doing so, autonomous networks reduce the cost, complexity and speed of managing a growing complex ecosystem of 5G services – as well as driving more frequent and more business-aligned optimization across the network than has ever been possible.

- **Customer experience is enhanced:** Autonomous networks monitor service degradation patterns and take corrective actions before they impact customer experience. In addition, smarter and frequent hyper-automated interactions between customers, business teams and the network ensure that issues get solved faster and services feel more responsive.
- **Resource efficiency is driven by business goals:** Autonomous networks ensure that the allocation of resources is in line with the larger business goals so that capacity ends up in areas that have the greatest impact. This translates into network actions that harness smarter resource- and energy use, creating more efficient operations that drive key business objectives.
- **Guarantee SLA commitments at scale:** Autonomous networks combine intent management with SLA assurance to guarantee the right performance, in the right place, at the right time and at scale. Service-specific intents make this possible, continuously monitoring and triggering actions that maintain SLA compliance.

4.2.3 The AI Pillars of Autonomous Networks

Autonomous systems need AI based framework that assists service operation, integration, creation and assurance processes at run time in a non-disruptive fashion.

Talk to Network refers to a framework that integrates AI tools to support autonomous network operations.

Knowledge and agent-oriented techniques are combined in the framework of the Talk to Network that converts natural language into actionable intelligence.

The Talk to Network framework transforms interactions with OSS/BSS and network domains, enabling various tasks and processes by utilizing three AI technology pillars of autonomous networks:

- Conversational AI
- Agentic AI
- Intent-based AI

The combination of these pillars results in an integrated system that can converse, orchestrate, break down intent, and execute it autonomously.

- **Conversational AI:** Conversational AI, powered by generative AI and large language models, enables natural context-aware communication between humans and machines, as well as between machines. It decodes language, knows intent and creates explainable reactions, which enable communication with complex systems. It is also used to enable the collaboration between agents and planning of tasks between the agents, combining human involvement with autonomous automation in managing a telecom network.
- **Agentic AI:** The agentic AI is designed to give autonomous agents the ability to sense, think and act independently, which is essentially a cohesive system with the potential to dynamically adapt. All these agents cooperate, adapt dynamically, and communicate, solve problems, and coordinate with the help of tools such as reinforcement learning and large language models. This has the effect of producing a flexible, intelligent system that can allow complex objectives to be handled with less human supervision.
- **Intent-based AI:** Intent-based AI acts as the coordination layer that translates high-level goals into clear, actionable steps for autonomous systems. To do this, it breaks down user

or business intents into smaller tasks, aligning them with the right agents or system functions to ensure everything works toward a common objective. Together with conversational and agentic AI, it translates high-level intents into actionable steps by turning broad goals into structured, executable plans.

4.2.4 Autonomous Architecture

An autonomous network is subdivided into autonomous domains according to the generic architecture proposed by TM Forum. Autonomous domains are allocated within layers of the network operation software stack, residing on the business, service or resource layer. Within a layer, multiple autonomous domains may exist in parallel or in further subordinate layers, each with terminal goals that it is required to meet and optimize. To reach its goals, it also needs other domains to contribute to and comply with certain requirements.

Intent is used to communicate and manage these requirements in the various layers Intent is managed using a layered approach. An intent manager assumes the role of owner when defining requirements that other domains must comply with. If, on the other hand, it receives requirements that it must comply with in its own domain, it assumes the role of intent handler.

The role of intent at each layer:

- **The business layer:** At the business layer, intent captures customer expectations and business goals, replacing traditional service level objectives (SLOs) with dynamic, goal-driven requirements. These intents are defined during service ordering and negotiated through APIs, then passed to the service layer for fulfillment. In this case, the emphasis is made on intent-based assurance, which tracks the performance of services, anticipates the SLA breach, and implements corrective measures according to the business worth.
- **The service layer:** Transforming business intents into actionable service and resource requirements is done at the service interface. In this case, the service orchestrator implicitly chooses and sets up services on the basis of intent. Monitoring of compliance is constant in the system and the system only intervenes when requirements are not fulfilled. This layer allows service logic to be decoupled with particular resources to enable more flexible or AI-driven orchestration. It allows autonomous real-time healing, service and optimization as well as guaranteeing that services change as the conditions and demands change.

- **The resource layer:** In the network domains in the resource layer, intent is handled at two levels: the management layer and the network function layer. For example, the RAN domain's intent manager ensures compliance with service-layer requirements using analytics, orchestration and AI agents. If deemed necessary, existing service instances can be reshaped to use new or more efficient resources. Intent-aware RAN functions monitor real-time performance and adjust configurations or control loops to meet evolving requirements. This and similar implementations for the other network domains enable the network to self-optimize and evolve based on overarching business objectives.

4.2.5 The AI pillars of autonomous networks

Autonomous systems require an AI-driven framework that supports service operation, integration, creation and assurance processes in a non-disruptive manner at run time. Talk to your network is an umbrella term that brings together key AI technologies and enablers to establish autonomous networks capable of addressing those areas.

The talk to your network framework integrates knowledge and agent-driven methods to transform natural language into actionable intelligence. Talk to your network completely changes the way you can interact with OSS/BSS and the network domains to drive different types of tasks and processes, as it leverages, as it leverages three AI technology pillars of autonomous networks: generative AI, agentic AI and intent-based AI. Together, these pillars contribute to an integrated system capable of conversation, orchestration, intent decomposition, and autonomous execution.

- **Conversational AI**

Conversational AI, powered by generative AI and large language models, enables natural context-aware communication between humans and machines, as well as between machines themselves. It interprets language, understands intent, and generates explainable responses, helping users interact with complex systems more intuitively. This technology also supports agent-to-agent collaboration and task planning, bridging human input with intelligent automation in areas like telecom network management.

- **Agentic AI**

Agentic AI empowers autonomous agents to sense, think and act independently, functioning as a cohesive system capable of dynamic adaptation. These agents collaborate, adapt in real time, and use tools like reinforcement learning and large language models to communicate, solve problems, and coordinate tasks. This results in a flexible, intelligent system capable of handling complex objectives with minimal human oversight.

- **Intent-based AI**

Intent-based AI acts as the coordination layer that translates high-level goals into clear, actionable steps for autonomous systems. To do this, it breaks down user or business intents into smaller tasks, aligning them with the right agents or system functions to ensure everything works toward a common objective. Together with conversational and agentic AI, it translates high-level intents into actionable steps by turning broad goals into structured, executable plans.

4.3 Network Slicing and Dynamic Service Provisioning

5G and cloud-native architectures require networks capable of real-time adaptation to heterogeneous service requirements. Network slicing is a solution to this problem as it allows one physical network to be divided into several logical networks, each of which is optimized to support a particular service, application, or performance goal.

In the autonomous network and zero-touch provisioning context, network slicing is no longer a design concept. It serves as the basis of dynamic service provisioning, in which network resources are automatically instantiated, scaled, and optimized on intent, policies and dynamic circumstances. Services can be dynamically created and updated automatically rather than configured manually through hard-coded definitions.

Dynamic service provisioning makes sure that the service requirements of individual network slices are consistently available to satisfy applications of ultra-low latency or massive IoT connectivity or consumer services with high throughput. Autonomous networks can be used to control the entire lifecycle of network slices, including their creation, assurance, and termination, and this is possible by integrating automation, analytics, and closed-loop control that allow the autonomous networks to achieve truly zero-touch operations.

4.3.1 Managing Network Slices: Simplifying Complexity, Driving Capability

Network slicing lets operators set up multiple virtual networks on the same real infrastructure. Each network can be customized for a different use case to meet customer needs. The management of these slices might be challenging, but there are advanced methods available to help, such as end-to-end orchestration. Assisting with dynamic slice provisioning, autonomous service assurance, and open API-based control in multi-vendor, multi-technology environments, cloud-native, AI-powered management platforms can handle comprehensive slice lifecycle management across network domains:

- **Dynamic slice provisioning:** Automated processes to deploy and change slices quickly on demand to adapt to changing customer demands in real time.
- **Autonomous service assurance:** AI-powered closed-loop automation and orchestration to guarantee end-to-end and domain-level service level agreements (SLA), efficient resource allocation among slices, and the ability to guarantee an efficiently utilized network.
- **Open APIs:** APIs Uncovered APIs to manage and monitor each slice to ease operations in multi-vendor and multi-technology environments.

4.3.2 Automation Underpins Network Slicing

Automation is a crucial component of the 5G journey; end-to-end network slicing is complex enough to necessitate automation. This complexity is only bound to grow with the increase in the number and types of slices as time goes by. In turn, the field of automation expands as network slicing is not only developed into a traffic management tool, but also an end-to-end and dynamic service framework, and integrated more deeply into the network operating and service provisioning.

The network slicing is generally deployed in phases by the communication service providers, with the first phase focused on small slices in the core or RAN networks, and the subsequent phases, as the operations become more mature, adopting full end-to-end slices. The first one is that CSPs maintain a small and fixed number of slices over time, and introduce slicing either in the core or in the RAN. On their 5G journey, CSPs add more slices, associate them with particular customers, places, and services, and transition to end-to-end slicing to achieve customer SLAs and make the best use of the network assets. At this stage, CSPs in a position to present network slicing as a service, real-time service provisioning and predictive functionality to ensure that they are able to satisfy the needs of their clients.

4.3.3 Dynamic Network Slicing

Service orchestration and lifecycle management of network slices is essential to the communication service providers (CSPs) to scale network slicing business and to leverage the 5G opportunity.

As CSPs commercialize their 5G networks and begin to expand their network slicing business, they expand the quantity and types of slices to address the needs of different industries. Scalable management necessitates service orchestration and network slice lifecycle management.

Dynamic network slicing solutions are modular, pre-integrated, and use-case-driven, enabling CSPs to manage, orchestrate, and assure the entire slice lifecycle seamlessly, while supporting automation and real-time service provisioning to capitalize on 5G opportunities.

4.3.4 Dynamic Service Provisioning at the Optical Edge

The primary emphasis of modern access networks, whether they are leased lines or legacy data services, has been on connection. An underlying transport network divides several types of traffic into time slots so that service vehicles can travel to their respective destinations. These forms of traffic include ATM, frame relay, Internet Protocol (IP), and time-division multiplexing (TDM). A minimum of four distinct networks are backed by a minimum of four distinct provisioning and management systems, as well as four distinct switching and routing components. A shift toward service-oriented and dynamically provisioned network architectures is required because bottlenecks in urban networks might be caused by devices' limitations on fixed-bandwidth connections.

But these TDM networks are so big that it take a long time to make them more modern. Also, any equipment used in this shift must support and improve SONET/SDH functions that are already in place. If service providers want to keep their investments from getting stuck, they need to make sure their networks can talk to each other and have a plan to upgrade to an infrastructure that is better at handling data and services. Even while carriers and service providers make most of their money from traffic carried by inefficient old TDM networks, the rollout of new services is still painfully sluggish. Hence, service providers are aiming to switch from time-division multiplexing (TDM) networks and manual provisioning models to service-based networks and dynamic, service-oriented methods of provisioning.

The provider's ability to differentiate itself solely through technology is now obsolete. The commodity status of bandwidth and access has resulted in low profit margins. Internet service costs have decreased dramatically over the years, reflecting the commoditization of bandwidth and the growing importance of operational efficiency in service delivery.

Companies with a substantial IT expenditure were previously the only ones eligible for T1 (1.554 Mbit/sec) lines. For a fraction of the cost of a T1, DSL offers comparable capability, therefore small businesses and homes across America are already yearning for the service. Carriers are under immense pressure to reduce the prices of bandwidth services since they are still an essential component of many products. Fast bandwidth service provisioning and modification is also required of them. The transition to value-added services is an important one, but they also need to safeguard their investments and make the most of their bandwidth.

4.4 Zero-Touch Configuration and Service Activation

Zero-touch configuration and service enablement is concerned with the automation of network service enablement. As NFV, SDN, and cloud-native networks become part of the networks, simplification and automation of operations processes become necessary. The result of this change is the implementation of zero-touch operations wherein services are defined and automatically enabled after being defined.

Zero-touch architecture enables newly defined services to be offered to the customers without operator involvement. The functions of providing services, activation, and assurance are performed using automated processes that make sure that the network is consistent, fast, and precise. This minimizes the complexity of the operations and retain the service reliability.

Zero-touch service activation allows subscribers to change the services quickly and easily. Upon a subscriber with the help of a customer service channel, online portal or self-care application ordering or upgrading a service, the service is automatically provisioned, activated and guaranteed. The records of subscribers and billing are updated and the device of the customer is provisioned with the necessary configuration in a short period of time and without any human intervention.

4.4.1 Service Provisioning and Activation in Telecom

Pre-integrated with Service Fulfillment and Orchestration, enabling coordinated activation procedures across multiple platforms, it supports the provisioning of converged services and intricate value-chain products. The solution gives operators a leg up in the telecom service provisioning and activation game by facilitating painless integration and rapid rollout of new goods and services.

Service activation frameworks employ multi-protocol mediation software that can be configured via graphical interfaces, enabling endpoints and network elements to support automated, standards-compliant service activation. A wide variety of endpoints, systems, and network nodes can be converted into a TMF-compatible Service Activation component using this capability.

4.4.2 Zero-Touch Automation in Autonomous Telecom Networks

A global consortium of telecom service providers began working on what would become known as Network operations Virtualization (NFV) standards for the virtualization of telecom networking operations in 2012.

The original intentions of network functions virtualization (NFV) were to use software, virtualization, commodity servers, and open standards to decrease network operational expenses (OPEX) and speed up the deployment of new revenue-generating services in response to service providers' intense pricing pressure and the ever-increasing demand for network bandwidth.

In the early days of NFV, some of these business goals were met. However, service providers have realized that to achieve their long-term goals of providing end-users with compelling experiences through efficient operations powered by modern technologies, they need to make even more drastic advances. "Zero-Touch Automation" (ZTA) is currently the industry's hot topic.

"Zero-touch provisioning" and "zero-touch deployment" are well-known phrases that describe the automation of data center and IT infrastructure. In the telecom business, ZTA takes this idea of automation a step further by encompassing the whole network operations lifecycle, from design and delivery to onboarding and monitoring as well as updates and decommissioning. With ZTA, telecom networks transition from their current state of partial autonomy to a state of complete autonomy, resulting in increased revenue and decreased operational expenses.

The service planning process today is largely manual in most cases and as such is quite prone to error and thus very time-consuming to most service providers. Under ZTA, the customers are able to state directly their requirements of services in digital interfaces and service design, order entry and performing their integration in the supply chain are automatically processed. The tasks which used to take weeks now can be accomplished in a few minutes with less risk of making mistakes.

The necessity to have common frameworks and interoperable mechanisms grows as the concept of the zero-touch configuration and service activation becomes a requirement in autonomous network operations. The vendors and multi-domain environments cannot be end-to-end automated consistently without proprietary implementations. This forms a very good addiction to standardized methods of defining how zero-touch processes are modelled, integrated and implemented through the network lifecycle.

In this regard, industry created standards organizations are instrumental in facilitating zero-touch at scale. The European Telecommunications Standards Institute (ETSI) contributes to this effort by developing standards that support automated configuration, service activation, and lifecycle management. These standards provide structured ways of working, reference architectures, and interface definitions that align with the objectives of zero-touch network operations.

4.4.3 ETSI Standards Types and Ways of Working

Understanding basic terminology is essential for following the ETSI standardization process.

Work Items (WI) are documents created through a cooperative and iterative development by group members and are, in the future, supposed to be made into standards.

Normative or informative Standards in ETSI may be either of the following:

- Normative standards are normative and stipulate conditions with which one has to comply.
- Informative standards are informative and explain issues describing the most important technological concepts.

The most common types of standards are:

- Specification for Technical Elements (TS), including Normative Elements;
- Report (TR) on technical matters, including informative material;
- Group Specification (GS), with normative content;
- Group Report (GR), with informative content.

The standards are written based on contributions submitted by professionals from any member company. Normative contents must be submitted for discussion and are accepted based on consensus. Each work item has an appointed person responsible for integrating all the approved contributions and managing the drafting, editing and approval processes. In meetings, remote and face-to-face, each contribution is presented by its authors and feedback is received from all participants.

4.5 Integration of AI with Autonomous Network Control

One of the key themes highlighted in recent industry discussions is the vision of "connecting everything." The next-generation networks are projected to provide billions of mobile subscribers and a growing number of connected devices with varying quality of service (QoS) levels to users with different service needs and price points in real time. This development adds much complexity to the network and introduces novel difficulties to network management and control. In order to overcome this heterogeneity and demand variability of dynamic services, the networks have to develop into higher degrees of autonomy.

In order to implement autonomous networks, operators need to adopt Artificial Intelligence (AI) and Machine Learning (ML) in the operational of the network. Although automation has already allowed improving the efficiency in the operations, AI and ML go beyond the set rules and algorithms. The AI/ML systems are capable of handling vast amounts of network data, detecting patterns, generating insights and formulating the correct action based on the existing conditions of the network.

AI/ML techniques can be applied to:

- Ascertain the relationship between the variables and the reasons behind the network's actions
- Predict the state of the network in the future so that preemptive decisions can be made
- Define a target network state and respond autonomously in response to local conditions
- Provide varying degrees of quality of service to end-user devices to make services more personalized.

Regardless of these benefits, the implementation of autonomy via AI/ML poses operational risk since decisions and control actions can be implemented without involving human intervention.

Deep Q Learning is one of the advanced learning techniques that entail exploration of the network environment until optimum actions are attained. To curb the risk, more AI methods may be used. The generative Adversarial Networks may be applied to generate a learned image of the network that is trained over the past data. This depiction is a digital twin, which enables the testing of AI-driven actions and validation of the activity offline and then implementing the same in the live network.

The deployment of AI/ML technologies is not all that is needed to build autonomous networks. The operators should also form a cross-functional team. The domain experts of Telecom domain establish the nature of operational issues and find the pertinent data. The data scientists take raw network data and convert them into machine-readable form and train and verify through appropriate learning algorithms. Cloud experts assist in gathering data in large quantities and develop automation systems that enable AI/ML systems to provide control measures in the network.

The successful application of AI in telecom operations also requires the establishment of an environment that facilitates cooperation in these areas. The dissimilarity in the background and problem-solving methods should be reconciled by common goals and harmonized processes. This kind of alignment is necessary in order to convert AI-driven insights into trustworthy autonomous network control.

4.5.1 Benefits of Agentic AI in Telecom Operations

The actual worth of the Agentic AI in telecom depends on the way the capabilities can be translated to actual business results to the operators.

Users to some extent achieve flexibility and agility previously unavailable to rule-based automation by operating intent-driven AI agents enabled by the natural language understanding of Generative AI.

Rather than responding to problems when they arise, AI-based automation enables networks to foresee and organize responses across domains and address incidents before customers experience any effect.

There are some significant advantages associated with this movement towards autonomous networks:

- Enables translation of agentic AI capabilities into measurable business outcomes for telecom operators
- Introducing Generative AI-enhanced intent-driven AI agents for decision-making and natural language understanding
- Improves operational flexibility and agility beyond traditional rule-based automation systems
- Shifts network operations from reactive fault handling to proactive issue anticipation and prevention
- Coordinates intelligent responses across multiple network domains
- Resolves incidents before service degradation is perceived by end users
- Supports the transition from automated operations to fully autonomous network control

4.5.2 Traditional AI & Automation vs. Agentic AI in Telecom

The main idea behind agentic AI is to integrate AI agents into telecom that have far more autonomy than previous AI models with automation in terms of thinking, planning, and acting. These individuals or entities:

- **Interpret intent:** Requests like "investigate latency spikes" are understood and the next steps are determined independently, rather than following established scripts.
- **Plan and sequence actions:** They are able to manage complicated, multi-step workflows, find the right data sources, correlate findings, and carry out duties correctly.
- **Learn and adapt:** They get better at reasoning and making decisions over time with the help of reinforcement learning and constant feedback.

Telecom Operational Capabilities	Traditional AI + Automation	Agentic AI
Decision-making model	Rule-based logic or static ML models	Intent-driven reasoning by autonomous agents
Adaptability	Predefined behavior, low adaptability	Self-adaptive via reinforcement learning and context

Scope of operation	Siloed (RAN, core, OSS, etc.)	Cross-domain and end-to-end orchestration
Response to anomalies	Reactive (alarms trigger workflows or tickets)	Proactive (agents identify and resolve issues before impact)
Workflow management	Hardcoded sequences or RPA flows	Self-directed planning and execution of multi-step tasks

4.5.3 How the Agentic AI Framework Works in Telecom

The fundamental component of Agentic AI is an agent-based architecture with a layer structure and AI agents endowed with the capabilities to perceive, reason, and act. All in real time. Instead of being used as independent tools, in telecom, these agents interact across domains to provide autonomous network functioning.

The Agentic AI model works in the following way:

1. **AI agents:** The domain-specific agents are specialized and work on different tasks, like anomaly detection, RCA, optimization, or remediation. Each collaborates alone in its area of specialization, yet reaches out to others in bigger multi-agent teams in order to provide end-to-end results.
2. **Perception layer:** This layer is a continuous data collector and normalizer of data that is collected throughout the network (telemetry feeds, alarms, event logs, policy states, and ticketing systems) and makes this data accessible to agents giving them the real-time visibility they require to determine the health of the network.
3. **Reasoning engine:** The reasoning engine is the brain of the system, as it is a logic-based model with ML that is used to analyze the current situation, find possible courses of action, and find the most effective next steps depending on the intention of the operator.
4. **Orchestration layer:** The layer ensures that the different agents are coordinated and that tasks are sequenced in order, dependencies taken care of, and that tasks always remain in line with the business goals of the operator.
5. **Action layer:** The action layer implements remediation measures on the network or provides action recommendations to the engineers or external systems once decisions have been made.

4.5.4 Challenges of deploying and operating autonomous intelligent networks

Transitioning to an autonomous intelligent network presents significant challenges for service providers, but potentially yields significant opportunities. Understanding both is crucial for a successful strategy:

- **Technical complexity and integration**

Autonomous operations require the integration of a variety of systems, including traditional operational support systems and business support systems (OSS/BSS), new AI and analytics platforms, orchestrators, and domain controllers. As many service providers suffer from fragmented systems, toolsets and standalone data, this presents a foundational challenge of unifying data management across the network.

A related challenge is the shortage of off-the-shelf automation components for critical functions, including intent engines and cross-domain orchestrators. This is a nascent area, with emerging technologies and approaches that are not yet widely deployed. Service providers often have to build custom solutions, or integrate multiple vendor-specific solutions, both of which increases complexity.

- **Conventional infrastructure and processes**

Service provider networks are typically a mix of outdated physical network elements (e.g., 4G/3G systems) and cloud-native functions (e.g., 5G). Older systems may not support the telemetry or dynamic configuration interfaces needed for closed-loop autonomous intelligent networks.

Additionally, service provider change management processes have historically been cautious and manual so as to avoid outages. Moving to intent-driven changes and automated remediation can clash with existing practices and culture. Service providers often cite traditional mindsets and processes as an obstacle towards automation. The network can not be autonomous if the organization insists on manual checkpoints at every step.

- **Organizational and skills gaps**

Autonomy demands a new skillset in the service provider workforce, shifting toward data scientists, automation engineers, AI specialists, and fewer command line interface (CLI) configuration-type of personnel. Most service providers have a critical skills shortage in areas such as artificial intelligence and machine learning (AI/ML), and also need to adapt their organizational structure to become cross-domain to facilitate effective automation.

Breaking down traditional silos of the radio access network (RAN), core, and transport teams is needed to foster an automation culture. However, organizational inertia can be high, with staff potentially resisting due to fear of job losses. Therefore, change management and upskilling programs are essential, but can be challenging to execute at scale.

- **Trust, transparency, and regulation**

Handing control to algorithms raises questions of trust and accountability. Ultimately, service providers have to ensure AI does not make a bad decision that causes an outage, as networks have become business critical and form an integral part of society and economies. In order to build trust, there is a need for explainable AI in operations so that humans understand why an autonomous agent or process made a decision.

Regulatory bodies in some countries may also require a level of human oversight, especially in areas affecting safety (e.g., emergency communications). Also, an autonomous network could potentially react to a cyberattack faster than humans, but if proper security is not in place, the automated closed-loops could be targets for exploitation (e.g., feeding false data to AI to mislead it). Thus, comprehensive governance and security frameworks must be in place.

- **Uncertainty of investment and return on investment (ROI)**

Implementing autonomous networks requires substantial investment in new systems, including AI platforms, data lakes, orchestration software, and the overhaul of existing processes.

ROI and timeline is often difficult to quantify, as they accrue with time, reduced OPEX, fewer outages, and an accelerated time to revenue for new services. Telco service providers can struggle to build a solid business case to justify the move towards an autonomous intelligent network, especially as most have invested heavily on 5G spectrum and deployments.

4.6 Edge Computing and Ultra-Low Latency Services

Edge computing is a distributed computing model that moves the enterprise applications nearer to the data sources like IoT devices or local edge servers. Such closeness to the data at its source can provide solid business advantages, such as the ability to gain knowledge more quickly, a higher response time, and an increased bandwidth option.

The fast multiplication and the growing computing capabilities of the IoT devices have also led to huge volumes of data. The volume of data is increasing with the 5G networks that are adding more mobile devices. The aim of cloud and AI technologies has been to automate and speed up innovation through the creation of actionable information of data. However, connected devices generate data on a scale and level that dwarfs network and infrastructure capacity.

Transmission of all the data generated by the device to a central data center or the cloud creates a problem of bandwidth and latency. The alternative provided by edge computing is more efficient- the data is calculated and analyzed in a place where it is generated. Due to the fact that data is not sent across a network to a cloud or data center to be processed, latency is minimized. Edge computing, with mobile edge computing in 5G networks, enables processing data nearer to its source and has a shorter latency, better response times and provides timelier and context-aware insights.

The amount of time that passes between a user's request and its completion is known as latency in the field of information technology. There is always a discernible lag time in any process, no matter how quick it appears. The company has made the reduction of such delays a priority. The ability to execute quickly and smoothly is essential for many applications that rely on low latency to enhance the user experience and contribute to customer satisfaction. Online meeting apps, mission-critical computation apps, and apps housed on the cloud are all examples of this type of application.

The difference between milliseconds and nanoseconds is the unit of measurement for ultra-low latency. Consequently, compared to low latency, ultra-low latency provides a substantially quicker response with significantly fewer delays.

A software-defined platform, smart network interface cards, programmable network switches, and software applications based on field-programmable gate arrays (FPGAs) are used to improve latency for new deployments.

4.6.1 Use cases for low latency

Low latency is important for any use case where a lot of data needs to go over the network. Included in this category are data and applications housed in the cloud, on the edge, or in a data center, all of which have increasingly complicated networking paths with multiple possible latency causes.

- **Online meetings:** Low latency is essential for modern interactive video conferencing and online meeting apps. User interaction is clumsy unless there is a noticeable lag time between spoken words and live video. Consequently, people talking over one another, which might lead to misunderstandings.
- **Online gaming:** Transmissions from third parties, or other players, are an integral aspect of gaming, and they might be located anywhere in the globe. Furthermore, there needs to be a live-action sensation to the fast-paced action and interactivity.
- **Low latency trading:** The goal of low latency trading in the financial markets is to obtain information faster than other traders by taking advantage of millisecond advantages in network speed and latency.

A key component of low-latency trading is the drive for trading businesses to have the fastest infrastructure and, more crucially, to locate their operations as close to the trading exchange as possible to minimize latency caused by distance.

Combining low-latency trading with algorithmic trading, often known as high-frequency trading, is a common strategy in programmed trading. This method has inspired the creation of whole trading firms; rumor has it that 70% of the NY Stock Exchange's daily volume is programmed trading.

4.6.2 Elements of Low Latency Networks

A significant gain in network performance can be achieved by reducing latency through a combination of minor improvements and time savings in multiple areas. Some of the possible enhancements are:

- **Programmable Network Platform:** Network latency and other networking issues can be easily addressed by developers and engineers using the programmable network platform to build and release new features, upgrades, and applications.
- **Smart Network Interface Cards (Smart NICs):** The Smart NICs can be programmed on an FPGA and have the software flexibility and features to support designs with very low latency and high performance.

- **Firmware Development Kits:** An FPGA-based programmable switch or Smart NIC can have application-specific intelligence and functionality added to it with the help of a firmware development kit (FDK).
- **FPGA Devices and Software:** Software and field-programmable gate array (FPGA) devices can be set up to work in certain ways that cut down on delay and solve today's tough network problems.
- **Storage Area Network:** Storage area networks (SANs) enable users to access data stored in data centers from anywhere in the world using a subnetwork of storage devices that are shared across a high-speed network.
- **IT Operations Management (ITOM) Platform:** Computing, networking, and application resource management (ITOM) software consolidates all the necessary tools for provisioning, managing, and monitoring the performance, status, and delivery of these resources.

4.6.3 Key capabilities for edge computing

The selected solution should make it possible to achieve the following objectives, regardless of the kind of edge computing (cloud, Internet of Things, or mobile edge).

- **Distribute software efficiently at scale:** Deploy software only when it's needed, cut down on wasteful administration, and save money.
- **Use open-source technology:** Use an edge computing option that encourages new ideas and can work with all the different kinds of devices and equipment on the market today.
- **Address security concerns:** Make sure that the appropriate workloads are executed on the appropriate machine in the correct order. Verify that the business's policies can be easily enforced.

4.6.4 Use cases for edge computing

Many different kinds of apps, goods, and services can make use of edge computing. Here are a couple of options:

Security System Monitoring

- **IoT devices:** Running code locally on Internet-connected smart devices, as opposed to on the cloud, can improve the efficiency of user interactions.

- **Self-driving cars:** The ability to respond instantly, without having to wait for server-side instructions, is essential for autonomous vehicles.
- **More efficient caching:** Application code executed on a content delivery network (CDN) edge network allows for content caching customization, resulting in more efficient user content delivery.
- **Medical monitoring devices:** Medical devices must be able to act right away, without having to wait for a cloud server to react.
- **Video conferencing:** Relocating backend operations closer to the video's source can reduce latency and lag since interactive live video consumes a lot of bandwidth.

4.7 Chapter Summary

In this chapter, the author discusses the history of Autonomous Networks and Zero-Touch Provisioning as the main features of next-generation telecom and enterprise networks. It presented the idea that network complexity, service diversity, and scale have been the main factors in making the traditional manual processes unviable, hence the necessity of automation and intelligence throughout the network's life cycle.

The main principles of autonomous networking were presented in the chapter and explained in relation to AI/ML, data analytics, and policy-driven control frameworks as the enablers of these capabilities. The concepts of self-configuration, self-optimization, self-healing, and self-protection were the main topics discussed in the chapter. Zero-touch provisioning as an operational model was characterized as a critical one that permits the deployment, configuration and management of network services and resources with the least intervention from human beings, thus considerably lessening the time taken for deployment and operational errors.

The examined chapter included key architectural features like closed-loop automation, intent-based networking, orchestration platforms, and integration with cloud-native as well as software-defined infrastructures. Practical use cases and benefits, including better agility, scalability, and cost-effectiveness, were discussed, along with the challenges of data quality, interoperability, security, and the necessity of trust in autonomous decision-making. Overall, the chapter drew attention to the fact that self-governing networks and zero-touch installation are not only facilities but very much enabling factors to the future services support, operational cost-effectiveness, and consistent high-quality user experiences in increasingly variable network environments.

Very Short Questions

1. Name one component of low-latency networks.
2. Which layer translates business intent into service actions?
3. What problem does zero-touch provisioning reduce in deployment?
4. What AI pillar enables natural language communication with networks?
5. Name one use case of edge computing.
6. What is zero-touch provisioning?
7. Name one benefit of autonomous networks.
8. What is the main goal of dynamic network slicing?
9. Which layer handles real-time resource management in autonomous networks?
10. What does intent-based AI do in autonomous networks?

Short Questions

1. How does AI/ML contribute to operational intelligence in networks?
2. Explain how intent is used in autonomous network management.
3. Mention two benefits of agentic AI in telecom operations.
4. Explain the concept of autonomous networks.
5. What challenges do CSPs face when managing multiple network slices?
6. Describe the role of the service layer in autonomous architecture.
7. Why is edge computing important for ultra-low latency services?
8. How does zero-touch provisioning reduce human error?
9. What are the three AI pillars in autonomous networks?
10. How does dynamic service provisioning work in network slices?

MCQs (Multiple Choice Questions)

1. **Which standardization body is instrumental in zero-touch network operations?**
   A. ISO
   B. ETSI
   C. IEEE
   D. ITU
2. **Agentic AI in telecom can:**
   A. Only follow predefined scripts

B. Plan, learn, and act autonomously across domains

C. Operate without reinforcement learning

D. Ignore business goals

3. **Network slicing allows:**

A. One logical network only

B. Multiple virtual networks on the same physical network

C. Manual traffic routing

D. Reducing automation

4. **Zero-touch provisioning primarily helps in:**

A. Increasing manual setup

B. Automatic deployment and configuration

C. Decreasing automation

D. Manual monitoring

5. **In autonomous architecture, the business layer primarily focuses on:**

A. Hardware optimization

B. Translating customer expectations into intents

C. Managing FPGA devices

D. Handling network errors only

6. **Dynamic service provisioning is driven by:**

A. Fixed network policies

B. Intent, policies, and real-time conditions

C. Manual configuration of each device

D. Random resource allocation

7. **Edge computing reduces latency by:**

A. Processing data closer to the source

B. Sending all data to a central cloud

C. Ignoring IoT devices

D. Delaying computations

8. **Which of the following is a key benefit of autonomous networks?**

A. Manual configuration

B. Reduced operational complexity

C. Slower service provisioning

D. Increased human intervention

9. The AI pillar responsible for translating high-level goals into actionable steps is:

A. Conversational AI

B. Agentic AI

C. Intent-based AI

D. Predictive AI

10. One challenge addressed by autonomous networks is:

A. Decreasing automation

B. Network complexity and SLA assurance

C. Limiting service diversity

D. Manual provisioning only

MCQ Answer sheet

Q1	Q2	Q3	Q4	Q5	Q6	Q7	Q8	Q9	Q10
B	B	B	B	B	B	A	B	C	B

Chapter 5: Security, Deployment Models, and Future Directions

5.1 Chapter Introduction

Many companies are currently upgrading their main integration systems or even putting their previous integration systems to the sidelines. In case of enterprise integration, however, integration of security and deployment methods was the most significant aspect that determined the success or failure of the project. The adoption of cloud-native platforms was quick and highly influential on the architectural design, selection of deployment model, and security. This is why the factors mentioned above should be thoroughly analyzed to make sure that it will be reliable, compliant, and scalable.

The consideration explores the key security principles required of the current integration platforms and also, in further detail, provides an insight of the standard deployment models in the industry namely, public, private, hybrid and multicloud. It also identifies models that can accommodate various organizational requirements in security, regulation compliance, performance, and cost efficiency.

5.2 Industry Deployment Models and Use Cases

Moving the workload to the cloud or installing another cloud environment allows organizations to obtain more out of the existing legacy systems. Nevertheless, different types of cloud deployments come with different features, advantages, and prices. Therefore, it is crucial for companies to analyze the various models of cloud deployment before taking the final decision about migration. We will discuss the various cloud computing deployment model types, their pros and cons, as well as present case scenarios to guide you through the decision of what is the best solution for your company.

5.2.1 Main Types of Cloud Deployment Models

1. The Public Cloud Deployment Model:

In a public cloud model, companies utilize shared cloud resources from a software company that provides cloud services (CSP) like Microsoft Azure, Amazon Web Services (AWS), or Google Cloud Platform (GCP). Although public cloud vendors provide the same fundamental set of services, knowing their specific abilities & pricing structures will help you determine which vendor is best for your requirements.

- **Benefits of Public Cloud:** Public cloud computing comes with the facility of being highly scalable, flexible, and cost-efficient. The majority of the companies will buy cloud resources through a pay-as-you-go approach which makes the deployment model perfect for changing or uncertain workloads.
- **Challenges of Public Cloud:** Public cloud platforms usually come with solid security features; however, companies have to consider the shared responsibility model as it allocates certain security measures to the provider and leaves the others to the customer. Firms that depend on a single cloud vendor for their services may also feel a sort of vendor lock-in, having difficulty switching one vendor's tools and services for another's.

2. The Private Cloud Deployment Model:

In the case of the private cloud model, the infrastructure is entirely reserved for one organization. A business can choose to install this deployment model in its own premises or let a third-party managed data center operate the model.

- **Benefits of Private Cloud:** Private cloud services allow for companies that desire to have a firmer grip on their infrastructure for reasons such as legacy systems or compliance requirements to have that grip. It is extremely flexible and can accommodate the requirements of more difficult migration and digital transformation projects.
- **Challenges of Private Cloud:** The initial costs of private cloud can be greater than those of public cloud installations. Companies may incur extra expenses for items such as hardware, data centers, people, etc. Organizations that want to control their own private clouds need to have highly skilled professionals to make sure that everything is set up and controlled correctly.

3. The Hybrid Cloud Deployment Model:

With at least one on-premises resource allocated along with a public cloud environment, hybrid models provide a middle ground between the utilization of public and private cloud resources. Businesses can take advantage of both environments' strengths; however, it can also complicate the challenges.

- **Benefits of Hybrid Cloud:** One of the main advantages of a hybrid cloud strategy is that it will provide the company with more choices regarding how to allocate its resources and distribute its workloads. The hybrid cloud can thus be a solution for companies that want to save on costs but still have a great level of control over their critical workloads at the same time.
- **Challenges of Hybrid Cloud:** It becomes harder for companies to make sure that their environments are slim if they have to deal with more places where they conduct their business. The hybrid cloud deployment has its complexities that must be planned well to be able to manage them.

4. The Multicloud Deployment Model:

The multicloud model is akin to the hybrid cloud, however, the major differentiator is that it comprises of more than one public cloud. A multicloud set-up can, for instance, be deployed to cater to various workloads or geographic areas.

- **Benefits of Multicloud:** The use of more than one public cloud results in a more robust environment, thus, the chances of getting out of service and business interruptions are reduced. When companies use several cloud providers, vendor lock-in becomes harder to happen. Flexibility is greatly increased because the companies can select the best cloud provider for their specific workloads and thereby, they reap the benefits of the increased flexibility.
- **Challenges of Multicloud:** In a similar way to hybrid cloud, management of several environments can be complicated, and the total cost of ownership (TCO) optimization can also be a problem with more options to choose from.

5.2.2 Use Cases for Different Cloud Deployment Models

The cloud deployment model that is best suited for a particular company will vary depending on a number of factors, such as the specific performance requirements of the application, security and compliance issues, and the company's cost management approach to achieving maximum resource efficiency and redundancy. Each deployment model has some typical use cases, and here they are:

- **Public Cloud Use Case**

Manufacturing businesses expand and modify their goods throughout time to satisfy changing consumer demands. The public cloud is intended to achieve the same goal. An Azure migration and a far more adaptable IT environment were the outcomes of a manufacturing company's search for an evolution-friendly solution to its outdated systems.

- **Private Cloud Use Case**

Large volumes of sensitive data are handled by healthcare institutions. In the wrong hands, personally identifiable health information might be harmful. Compared to a public cloud deployment, a private cloud offers a better degree of security and compliance with laws like HIPAA.

- **Hybrid Cloud Use Case**

In certain businesses, hybrid cloud deployments will be the best choice due to a trade-off between security and flexibility. When legacy systems need to be moved to an environment that offers greater customization than public cloud deployments, hybrid cloud becomes a possibility. One extraordinary instance we came across was that of an energy trading firm undergoing a divestment which needed a managed hybrid solution to be put in place for the future.

- **Multicloud Use Case**

For firms that do not require the compliance and security levels of a private cloud but seek additional redundancies, multicloud deployments can be a good choice. Companies with operations spread across various countries or regions might create a multicloud environment to have more geographical diversity in their workloads.

5.2.3 Benefits of Using Feature Flags in Cloud Environments

- **Enhanced Deployment Process**

Feature flags provide an opportunity for the developers to separate the launches of new functionalities from code releases, hence making it possible to have more frequent and dependable deployments. This also helps in lessening the risks and downtimes related to deployments, thus resulting in a much cozier deployment process.

- **Cost-Effectiveness**

By feature flags, organizations will be able to roll out the new functionalities on a small set of their users prior to the rollout. Such a gradual release policy will serve in identifying and correcting the problems as soon as possible and therefore, minimize the costs associated with the potential outages or uninstallation.

- **Upfront Control**

The feature flags provide the developers with a direct and immediate control of the releasing of the features because the developers can turn features on or off at any time, and without carrying out any code customizations or utility of the application. This flexibility promotes rapid experimentation and iteration and therefore, it takes a shorter time before new features are made available to users.

- **Use Cases**

The use of feature flags has multiple applications, including A/B testing, canary releases, dark launches, and a gradual rollout. Through these techniques, businesses can gather feedbacks on the users and serve as a basis when making decisions on features and also their performance as well as verify their assumptions.

- **Improved End User Experience**

One method of the gradual rollout of a feature is the use of feature flags which in turn guarantees that the user experience is continuous and seamless. The method also reduces chances of the born bugs or usability problems that may adversely affect retention and satisfaction of users.

The process of the deployment can be significantly enhanced by adding feature flags to the cloud deployment models, which would enable control, lower costs, and offer the end users a superior experience on the initial rollout. Cloud platform services and automation tools can help organizations to manage features in a more effective way and hasten the process of the application innovation.

5.2.4 Industry Deployment Models and Use Cases

Here are 6 important considerations when selecting the appropriate cloud deployment model:

1. **Assess Business Needs and Goals**
   - Identify specific requirements, such as cost-effectiveness, scalability, security, and regulatory compliance.
   - Consider factors like data sensitivity, workload characteristics, and geographic location.
2. **Evaluate Cloud Deployment Models**
   - Private Cloud: Opt for a private cloud deployment model if stringent security and compliance requirements are paramount, or if customization and control over

infrastructure are essential. Consider self-managed solutions or platforms like Microsoft Azure Stack for on-premises private clouds.

- Public Cloud: Choose a public cloud deployment model for cost-effective scalability, accessibility, and ease of use. Major providers like Amazon Web Services (AWS), Google Cloud, and Microsoft Azure offer multi-tenant environments suitable for the general public, with self-service capabilities and pay-as-you-go pricing models.
- Hybrid Cloud: Consider a hybrid cloud deployment model if flexibility and workload portability are key priorities. This model allows organizations to leverage both private and public cloud resources, ensuring optimal performance and resource utilization.

3. **Review Provider Offerings**
   - Assess the features, services, and support offered by cloud providers like Microsoft Azure, Google Cloud, and Amazon Web Services to ensure alignment with business needs.
   - Consider factors such as geographical availability, service-level agreements (SLAs), and integration capabilities when evaluating cloud providers.
4. **Consider Cost Implications:**
   - Evaluate the total cost of ownership (TCO) for each cloud deployment model, taking into account factors like initial investment, operational expenses, and potential cost savings.
   - Compare pricing structures, including subscription-based models, pay-as-you-go options, and reserved instances, to determine the most cost-effective solution.
5. **Scalability and Performance:**
   - Determine the scalability requirements of your workloads and applications, considering factors like peak usage periods, growth projections, and seasonal fluctuations.
   - Choose a cloud deployment model that offers scalability and performance capabilities to meet current and future needs, such as auto-scaling features and high-performance computing options.
6. **Security and Compliance:**
   - Prioritize security and compliance considerations when selecting a cloud deployment model, especially for industries with strict regulatory requirements.

- Evaluate the security features and compliance certifications provided by cloud providers, such as encryption, identity and access management (IAM), and industry-specific compliance standards.

5.3 Standardization and Open Network Architectures

The way into comprehending the importance of ORAN and network standardization in the world of 5G installations. It explains clearly how these factors play a vital role in making sure that different networks have the same features and can communicate with each other freely.

Open networking refers to a network that is based on open standards and cheap hardware. It is a broad term that characterizes a common practice of using open standards. In the case of open networking, a computer system may have open hardware and software components, compatibility, growth and expansion options.

Open networking is basically the same thing as open standards, which mostly aim at getting a common and public consensus on processes for interoperability and data exchange. An open network goes against the concept of a closed network, which restricts networks to a specific set of providers only.

5.3.1 Understanding Network Standardization

Getting to know the network standardization is very important for understanding the basic principle of consistency and interoperability together with 5G networks. Network standardization as a concept has mainly to do with the procedure of making and putting into practice a certain set of quarried, rules, protocols, and specifications which determine the way communication systems function within a network environment.

Among the primary ideas in network standardization is the development of universal frameworks which allow different parts of the network infrastructure to communicate with each other without any problems. The frameworks specify the protocols and operation of network elements like transmission protocols of data, addressing scheme and signaling protocols. The fact that both the network operators and equipment manufacturers adhere to these uniform templates allows the network operators and equipment manufacturers to ensure that their products and services will be compatible with those of the rest of the players in the eco-system thereby improving interoperability as well as ensuring that information can be easily transmitted between different network environments.

Another significant factor of the entire process of standardization was the establishment of the rules and specifications that defined the criteria of data transmission, processing, and interpretation within the network. The protocols were the principal factors in the communication between the network devices and it enabled data transfer in a manner that was reliable, effective, and secure. The 3rd Generation Partnership Project (3GPP) standards related to radio access, core network architecture, and service orchestration have been laid down along with the Internet Engineering Task Force (IETF) standards for Internet Protocol (IP) networking as the standardized protocols in connection to 5G networks.

Moreover, standardization attempts are to a great extent aimed at the setting up of checking procedures and certifying mechanisms for the network devices and service that would verify their conformity with the recommended standards and specifications. Checking for compliance means careful evaluation of product performance, features, and compatibility according to the given measurement, while certification is the guarantee offered to the parties involved that the product is up to the standard in terms of quality and compatibility.

In general, mastery of the basic principles of network standardization is a key factor in the construction of strong and dependable 5G networks capable of serving numerous different types of services and applications. Moreover, through the following of unified plans, rules, and definitions, the operators of networks and suppliers of hardware will have better compatibility, simplified installation and maintenance, and faster coming up with new technologies and ideas in the telecoms sector.

5.3.2 Core Concepts of Standardization

The core concepts of standardization with regards to network infrastructure are the basic principles and components that influence the creation, use, and care of standard protocols, tools, and specifications. The standardization concepts are the most important factors in achieving uniformity, interconnection, and trustworthiness in various parts of a network environment. Following are few essential core concepts of standardization:

1. **Protocol Standardization:** Protocols are rules and regulations that govern how networks' devices should interact. The standardization of protocols includes specifying a universal set of regulations for data transmission, acknowledgment, detecting and correcting errors, and other parts of the communication. Among the protocols that have been made standard are TCP/IP (Transmission Control Protocol/Internet Protocol) for communication over the network and HTTP (Hypertext Transfer Protocol) for browsing the web.
2. **Interoperability:** Interoperability is the capacity of different network parts, systems, and apps to talk to each other, share data, and function together with no issues at all. The standardization process makes sure that interoperability is accomplished by establishing the common interfaces, data formats, and protocols through which the different devices and systems can be effectively merged. This has the advantage of allowing diverse technologies to be integrated and also aids in the promotion of both compatibility and flexibility in the arrangement of the networks.
3. **Open Standards:** Open standards are specifications that are created and upheld through a consensus process by organizations or communities, such as the IEEE, IETF, and ITU. Open standards are available to everyone and come without charge for their application, thus assuring transparency, being easily accessible, and being widely adopted. They allow the innovation, competition, and collaboration among the participants and thus, create a scenario where the production and rendering of the interoperable products and services of the utmost quality are done.
4. **Compliance and Certification:** Compliance testing and certification programs check if the network equipment, devices, and services comply with the established standards and specifications. Compliance testing is a comprehensive process to evaluate product performance, functionality, and interoperability against the criteria laid down, which ensures that the products live up to the required quality and compatibility standards. Certification is an assurance to the stakeholders that the products have gone through the rigorous testing and validation process, which in turn, builds trust in the products' reliability and interoperability.
5. **Evolution and Adaptation:** The process of standardization is an ongoing undertaking that aligns with new technologies and new demands, including the trends of the industry at the moment. The standards bodies keep on changing and modernizing the prevailing standards

in order to meet the emerging challenges, accommodate the current technological developments, and address the evolving usage situations. Such a persistent process makes it sure that the standards are up to date, efficient, and flexible to the ever-changing nature of network environments.

5.3.3 How to define open networking

Open networking cannot be defined simply. The term might have different meanings in different communities. The term "open networking" can refer to a wide range of concepts, including the degree of network interoperability and component substitution.

Some may define open networking more narrowly, such as using open-source protocols for software-defined networking (SDN). Combining an open-source network operating system (OS) with hardware that is accessible to the public in a virtual machine is another example of open networking.

Additionally, vendors might signify different things when it comes to open networking. It might be described by a vendor as utilizing a collection of publicly available application programming interfaces (APIs) that interact with other tools or as adhering to current networking standards. Additionally, vendors describe open networking as the degree of transparency of their own network as opposed to external standards. White box networking is also related to the word.

5.3.4 Open Networking Examples

The term "open networking" refers to a wide range of applications. On the other hand, companies may manage less expensive hardware throughout a computer network by using an open-source controller operating system.

Comcast and ONF implemented the open-source program Trellis in September 2019. Trellis is an architecture pattern that creates fabrics for network services based on virtualization of SDN and network activities. Trellis uses an OpenFlow protocol, which serves as a southbound API, and an open source SDN controller.

Network switches can be instructed where to deliver packets by servers using the OpenFlow protocol. The control and forwarding layers of an SDN-based architecture are divided by OpenFlow, a common communication interface.

Each switch in a traditional network includes proprietary software that instructs it on what to perform. In contrast, packet-moving choices are centralized by OpenFlow. This implies that the network may be programmed independently of the specific switches and data center equipment.

5.4 Resilience, Fault Tolerance, and Reliability Strategies

The modern networked and distributed systems have the expectation of continuous operation regardless of failures, high traffic, and any other unpredictable circumstances. Therefore, the implementation of resilience, fault tolerance, and reliability strategies will be no less than a magic wand for drawing the line between the design life and the death of the system. Ultimately, these strategies will help the systems not only to survive and endure but also to be forgiving and demonstrate the right level of performance and availability in the process. Companies can smartly integrate redundancy, failover mechanisms and intelligent recovery to reduce the outage time, keep outages of service at bay and provide sound-network services.

5.4.1 The Importance of Resilience in System Design

At a good time, and a priori, faults should be anticipated to have been corrected.

- **Minimizing Disruptions and Downtime**: By definition, resilient systems reduce the impact of failures by their capability to predict failures as well as by taking action in advance of these failures. In reality, though, these systems are so sophisticated that they can promptly change their mode and operate even when they break, which will help decrease the number of time that all processes will be interrupted, as well as reduce the related expenses.
- **Maintaining Continuous Operations**: Robust systems are able to overcome and recover all forms of failure including hardware faults, software faults, or network failure and therefore, they ensure that important services are made available to the consumers without failures. The 24-hour operation is essential to the business because it can enable them to evade the expensive downtimes and to please their customers.
- **Ensuring Data Integrity and Recovery**: On the lines of defense, resilient systems have robust data backup and recovery practices, and they can therefore withstand loss and corruption of data. In addition, they are also able to continue accessing good data and providing business on a round-the-clock basis by periodically making backups and sharing the copies across different locations.

- **Protecting Against Cyber Threats**: By a huge margin, cyber-attacks are a big menace to the systems and data in this ever-digitalizing world. As an example, resilient systems being implemented possess potent security techniques such as encryption, authentication, and intrusion detection, which subsequently reduce the risk of intrusions and maintain the integrity and confidentiality of sensitive information.
- **Adapting to Change and Scaling**: The resilient systems should be built in a way that they become highly flexible and simultaneously undergo scalability in other words, they should be able to adapt as times, areas and workloads require. Those systems are capable of withstanding throws like the unexpected increase in traffic or combination of new technology by changing their functioning with regard to the new demands, making it dynamic and retaining the same level of performance and remaining equally reliable as it was earlier on.

5.4.2 Understanding the Fault Tolerance Challenge

Fault tolerance refers to the ability of a certain piece of equipment to continue functioning despite the failure of certain components of it. This cannot be done without complete understanding of the way the system behaves when pressure comes on and implementing the measures that will reduce the likelihood of occurrence of a risk. The following are some of the most critical cases of fault tolerance:

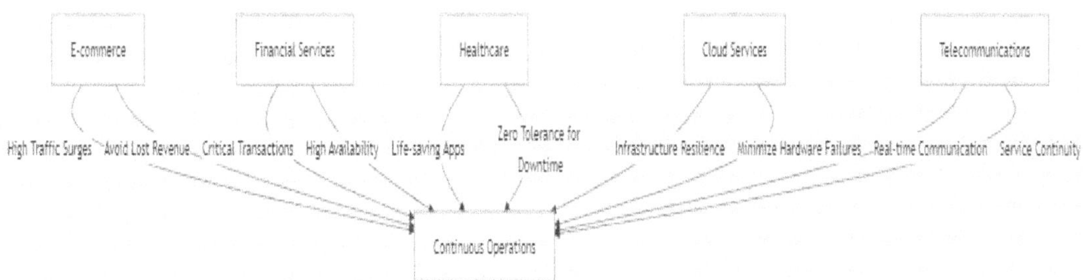

Figure 5.1: Business Drivers for Continuous Operations

Source: (Self- Created)

- **E-commerce**: In the case of sales events, it is important to ensure that your systems are capable of handling sudden influxes and their ability to continue working so that you do not lose on revenue.

- **Financial Services**: Systems in a transaction and account management environment should be accessible and hardy, in any event of failure.
- **Healthcare**: The support systems of activities that save lives have to be trustworthy- there should be no room to take a break.
- **Cloud Services**: Digital sphere is a battleground in which all the computers are dependent on each other to collaborate as a single chained set, which makes its best efforts to conquer the challenges that stand in its way.
- **Telecommunications**: There is never any chance of the user paying a stride in live communications; therefore, fault tolerance must be extended to all levels.

All sectors must ensure that they develop strategies to enable the systems recover fast once they have collapsed and at the same time offer reliable services to the end consumers.

5.4.3 Core Reliability Challenges in Distributed Systems

Fault tolerance does not merely relate to minimizing the down time of the systems, but also relates to the fact that the various components of a system are operating in a perfect cooperation with each other, despite the presence of failures. The continuously growing complexity and decentralization of systems provoke the appearance of the following dilemmas:

- **Service Failures**: This is where the network is affected, software bugs or hardware failures that result in the off-line of partially or all of the service components.

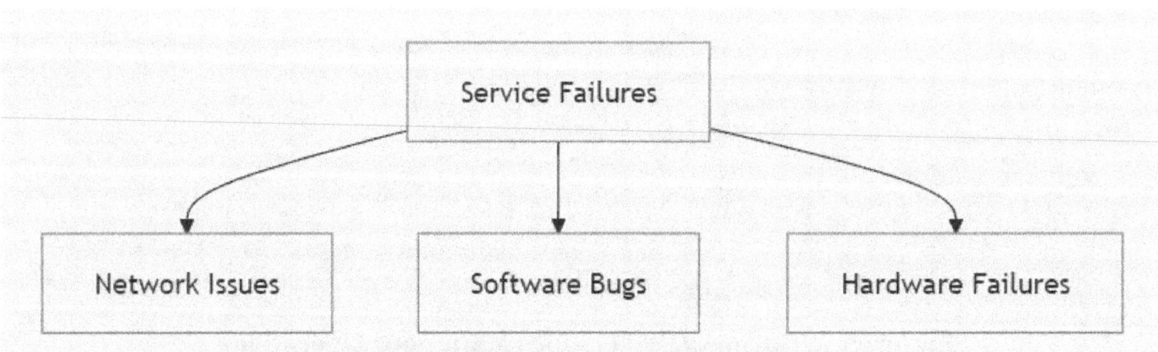

Figure 5.2: Service Failures

Source: (Self- Created)

- **Network Partitions**: The communication may be broken between some distributed systems resulting in the temporal availability of some parts.

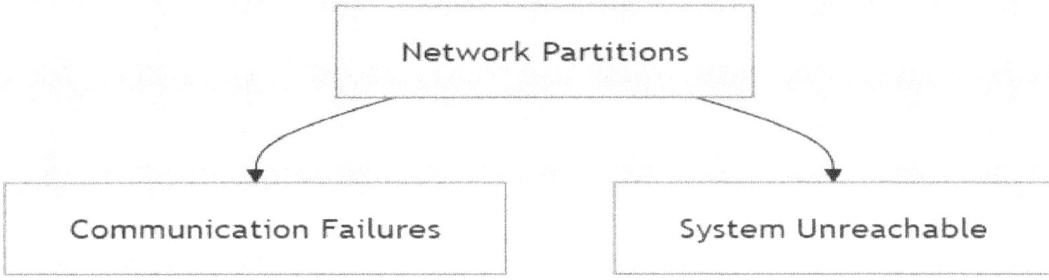

Figure 5.3: Network Partitions

Source: (Self- Created)

- **Data Corruption**: The fact that the data can be mixed up or corrupted due to the weakness of the storage systems or the issues in relaying the data hence the necessity to have powerful and trustworthy data integrity systems.

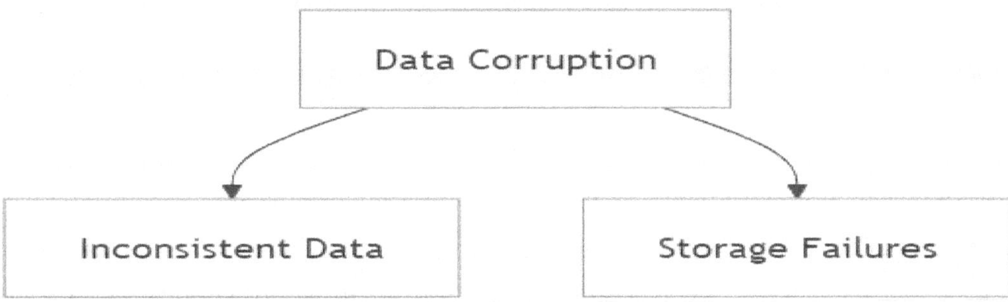

Figure 5.4: Data Corruption

Source: (Self- Created)

- **Latency and Timeouts**: The system latencies and timeouts experienced in failure situations are likely to diminish the user experience.

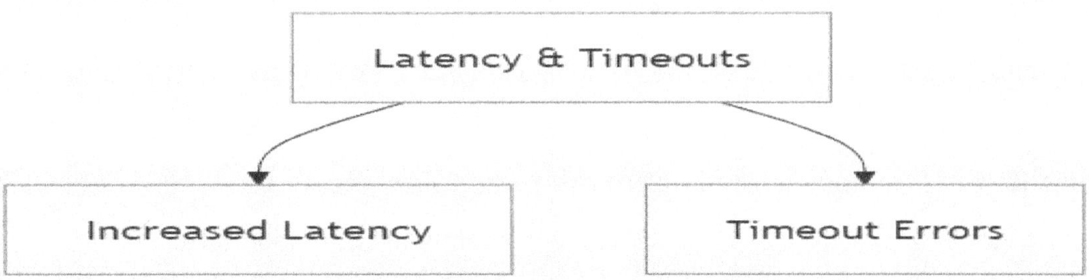

Figure 5.5: Latency & Timeouts

Source: (Self- Created)

5.5 Security Challenges in AI-Enabled Telecom Networks

Such applications as smart automation, predictive analytics, network optimization, and improved customer service are some of the ways AI is being used in the telecom industry. However, the security problems and threats associated with the use of AI have also emerged; hence, telecommunication network operators should discuss these issues in order to make their networks secure and quality.

5.5.1 The Security Risks of AI Adoption in Telecom Networks

The application of artificial intelligence (AI) to telecommunications industry has been increasing in a steady way and has many advantages that include the enhancement of the quality of networks, customer service enhancement, and cost-efficient operation. The application of AI to telecom networks has its difficulties, however, the issue of security also creates certain challenges in the field, which must be evaluated and avoided carefully.

The introduction of AI into telecom networks usually brings along cyber-attacks as one of the main security risks. The tricksters who eventually probe into the network security and exploit it will not only gain access to the AI systems which will be very intricate and deep-rooted in the network infrastructure but will also be able to manipulate the service or even extract confidential information by the use of the A.I. algorithm working in a predictive maintenance or network optimization scenario that is functioning to the fullest. For example, if an AI algorithm for predictive maintenance or network optimization is functioning just right, a hacker could still use it to either manipulate the process, thus causing a service disruption, or he could just go on stealing sensitive data.

Another safety issue that the AI systems might unknowingly inflict on the network is bias or error which would cause the network security to be compromised. The AI algorithms are trained on large amounts of data, and these data sets could be containing biases or inaccuracies which in turn produce unwarranted results. As an example, in case the AI that monitors the network to identify the anomalies has a failure, the good traffic will be mistaken as bad, which, in turn, will lead to unnecessary downtime or false alarms, and some of them will be, in fact, false.

Furthermore, people are concerned about the privacy of data and the fact that AI in telecom networks has to meet the requirements set by the General Data Protection Regulation (GDPR). In practice, AI use may demand enormous data volumes to work properly; hence, the issues of data processing, storage, and security emerge. The improper securing of sensitive data might result in costly data leaks and penalties from the regulatory authorities.

The intricate nature of systems powered by AI in telecom networks increases the risk of delays in the detection and reaction to security incidents. The application of conventional security methods such as firewalls and IDS (intrusion detection systems) may not be sufficient to resist the highly sophisticated attacks facilitated by AI. Therefore, it becomes paramount for telecom operators to set aside certain amount of funds of their budgets to get the skill of advanced threat detection and response which would enable them to protect their networks efficiently.

5.5.2 Challenges and Limitations of AI in Telecom

Telecommunication companies are widely incorporating artificial intelligence into their operations; however, the path is not full of difficulties. In this segment, we are going to take a glance at some of them.

- **Data Privacy and Security Concerns**

Telecom companies keep very sensitive customer data, for instance, call records and location information. When artificial intelligence works with this data, it is quite natural to question the access and the protection of such data.

The security lapses bring in more threats, especially when AI has the access to the crucial network infrastructure and in that case, the infrastructure can be targeted for cyber-attacks. One of the options is that firms can make the isolated testing environments to run the full security checks before the live deployment of the systems.

In addition, telecom operators are more and more applying rigorous data management policies which reduce the availability of AI systems to designated data. A lot of them make use of anonymization methods that make it possible to analyze the data for patterns without revealing personal information.

- **High Implementation Costs**

Using AI creates financial difficulties. A large amount of money will be spent on software and infrastructure, and in most cases, companies will have to replace their old systems with ones compatible with AI.

The smaller regional providers, especially, are the ones who have the hardest time handling these costs, thus widening the gap with bigger companies. The return on investment can be a slow process and very hard to quantify, hence it becomes difficult to validate the spending.

A few of the companies that want a good and easy AI transition gradually do it. On the other hand, others are centering AI in departments where they can immediately experience a profit increase through high-speed sales or low-cost operations, like taking care of customer service or doing predictive maintenance.

- **Talent Shortage and Skill Gaps**

The professionals who possess the know-how of both telecom_systems and Artificial Intelligence are scarce which as a consequence makes the implementation slow because the companies are all in for the same talent chase.

"The talent pool between_ engineers and_AI_experts is really difficult to spot," states a telco HR chief. Such mixed-up careers call_for the technical understanding of both domains.

In dealing with this issue, often companies invest in internal training, partner with universities, or offer incentives for staff to acquire AI skills. Others, however, are still dependent on vendors and consultants but this strategy can be costly in the long term.

5.5.3 Addressing challenges in AI implementation

Although AI offers tremendous opportunities in this sector, its implementation poses challenges for telecommunications companies. Here are some key considerations.

- **Data privacy and security**

AI systems are dependent on huge quantities of customer information, which consequently leads to discussions about user privacy and data security. Protecting user data and staying within the law are critical and thus proper safeguards are to be set up.

Furthermore, AI models demand data that is of the best quality and variety in order to give precise insights. Telecom firms are likely to face challenges like data silos, having partial data, and getting data from various sources. All these factors may result in the downgrading of the capabilities of AI algorithms and consequently, cause them to make erroneous predictions.

- **Integration with existing infrastructure**

Merging AI systems with the current telecom infrastructure can be a complicated and lengthy process. The telecom companies need to check that the existing systems are capable of supporting AI tech, and alienation of data should be done in a way that there is no interruption in the normal operation. Depending on the situation, it may take major investments in infrastructure renewing.

There's also cost and resource management. Telecom companies have to do a lot of deliberations between the benefits they might get and the costs they will incur besides doing an appropriate allocation of resources as part of their successful implementation.

- **Workforce transformation**

With AI taking on some of the tasks once performed by humans, a new challenge will arise in the form of training the employees to interact and utilize the capabilities of these systems effectively. In doing so, companies might have to provide the staff with upskilling and reskilling that will allow them to catch up with the new technology and methods. Telecommunications firms have no option but to bring on board training schemes to upskill their personnel with the right skills and know-how that will enable them to coexist with AI. Not only will this be a means to raise the level of workforce productivity, but it will also be a way for the employees to keep their position in a rapidly changing industry.

5.5.4 The Role of AI in Transforming the Telecom Industry

The market for AI in telecom is projected to reach $14.99 billion by 2027, driven by a compound annual growth rate (CAGR) of 42.6% from 2021. In other words, kapow. But why has the telecom industry in particular embraced AI with such wide-open arms? It all stems from a few very specific industry challenges that AI is very well suited to tackle:

1. **Complex Network Management**

As global traffic and network infrastructure expand, telecoms are finding that traditional management methods aren't cutting it. By automating routine tasks, AI enables operators to optimize their resources so they can handle those complex systems without having to hire half the population of their country. It's also helping operators offer the same resource-streamlining benefits to their customers. Take AI-driven call centers, for example: telecoms can equip businesses with thc tools to offer virtual assistants that can expedite the resolution of many of their customers' problems without the need for them to wait on hold. (Or for the businesses to expand their own call center staff.)

2. **The Constant Chase for Revenues**

AI can facilitate the development of new products and services, opening new revenue streams for telecoms. Deutsche Telekom, as one example, anticipates that AI will have contributed €1.5 billion in revenue from new offerings by 2027.

3. **Customer Expectations**

In a highly competitive market, customers will walk away if you deliver anything less than a seamless experience. AI helps telecoms personalize and accelerate services to improve that sense of customer satisfaction and prevent excessive churn. Approximately 62% of telecom providers are now using generative AI to enhance their customer experience. By 2027, that figure is expected to reach 90%.

4. **Fraud**

When you have fraud, you have revenue leakage. AI systems can detect and prevent fraudulent activities by analyzing patterns and anomalies in real time.

5. **Putting Data to Its Best Use**

This is the key to getting the most out of AI in telecom. You've heard the saying "garbage in, garbage out." Getting good outputs from AI depends on having good inputs. As it happens, telecoms tend to collect vast amounts of data from their users. If you — the human — can lean into analyzing what data you have, what data you can get, and how you can use it to equip customers with information they can really use, you can create some very compelling services just by learning how to ask AI the right questions. Think: Dynamic pricing. Predictive analytics to give an early warning about service outages. Automated, personalized offers that exactly match a given customer's usage needs. Sentiment analysis to uncover where your customer pain points are. Or: insert your amazing idea here.

5.5.5 Examples of AI Implementation in Telecom

Here's where the potential is hitting the pavement.

1. **Network Optimization: AI in Telecom Turns the Complexity into Simplicity**

Telecom networks are like living organisms, constantly shifting under the weight of billions of simultaneous connections. With the rollout of 5G and an explosion of IoT devices — forecasted to surpass 25 billion by 2030 — networks are facing unprecedented complexity. Traditional static management methods no longer suffice. The answer? Say hello to self-optimizing networks (SONs), powered by AI.

What are SONs?

In simple terms, self-optimizing networks use machine learning algorithms to monitor network traffic in real time, predict congestion points, and dynamically adjust network parameters. These systems enable telecom providers to optimize resources, improve reliability, and reduce downtime.

Why It Matters

Ericsson estimates that AI-driven network optimization improves operational efficiency by 15-20%. These systems also detect and resolve faults up to 50% faster, reducing service disruptions and protecting customer satisfaction.

AI in Telecom Case Study: Nokia's Manta Ray Cognitive SON

In June 2024, Nokia announced it had deployed a new cognitive SON for client STC Group to help the company boost its network efficiency. The company says its Manta Ray SON improved STC's network performance by up to 30% while reducing both energy consumption and the need for manual work.

2. Predictive Maintenance: AI in Telecom Keeps Companies Ahead of Failure

Telecom networks rely on extensive physical infrastructure, including cell towers, fiber-optic cables, and data centers. Maintaining this infrastructure is essential, but very, very costly. Worse, traditional reactive maintenance often results in downtimes. (Meaning: costly just got costlier.) Predictive maintenance uses AI to flip that script.

How It Works

AI systems monitor infrastructure in real time, analyzing performance data to detect anomalies. By identifying subtle changes that precede equipment failures, these systems allow operators to intervene before disruptions occur.

The Numbers

According to Deloitte, predictive maintenance can:

- Reduce downtime by 5-15%
- Lower maintenance costs by 20-25%
- Prevent up to 70% of unexpected failures

AI in Telecom Case Study: AI Protecting European Infrastructure

Vodafone and other European telecom operators have successfully used AI to monitor environmental stress on cell towers, such as extreme weather or wear and tear. These systems ensure uninterrupted service, particularly in remote or harsh conditions.

3. Fraud Detection and Cybersecurity: AI in Telecom Helps Defend the Frontlines

Telecom fraud is a growing menace, costing the industry over $45 billion annually. Scams like international revenue share fraud (IRSF), fake profiles, and identity theft are becoming more sophisticated, requiring equally advanced countermeasures. AI in telecom has some solutions.

How AI Is Helping to Prevent Fraud

AI excels at identifying anomalies in real-time network traffic. Machine learning models analyze behavioral patterns to flag suspicious activities, while automated systems can neutralize those threats immediately.

How It Might Hurt

While AI can help prevent fraud, it also introduces new challenges. Generative AI, capable of creating deepfakes and voice clones, is being weaponized by fraudsters. In response, telecom companies are racing to invest in AI systems that are capable of detecting synthetic content.

AI in Telecom Case Study: SK Telecom

SK Telecom deployed AI-driven cybersecurity tools that reduced cyber incidents by 25%. These systems continuously monitor network activity, predicting vulnerabilities and reinforcing security protocols before a breach occurs.

5.6 Future Research Trends in Autonomous Telecom Networks

At the moment, the telecom industry is undergoing a significant change that is characterized by a rapid technological innovation and the transformation of the business models. AI networks, cloud core architecture, satellite integration, and early research on upcoming wireless technologies such as 6G have grown into the most powerful factors influencing the making, setting up, and financial acceptability of modern networks. The operators have to deal with competition, declining margins, and the need to charge less for the same services at the same time. These developments have compelled the operators to reconsider the whole value generation and value maintenance process in the telecom ecosystem.

5.6.1 Future Trends in Intelligent Telco Network Automation

Over the last few years, the telecommunications sector has been largely relying on the implementation of autonomous networks in their infrastructure due to the increasing complexity of the telecom infrastructure. The networks are getting their operational performance bettered by the dependability of automation systems. One of the hot topics in automating smart networks is closed-loop automation that consists of the automated system granting real-time adjustments in operations by analyzing data continuously, which finally leads to better service quality and lesser downtime.

1. **Intent-Based Networking: Driving Proactive Optimization**

Old-style network operations are for the most part a response to events, meaning that human employees have to react to alerts, look into the problems, and carry out the repairs. Intent-based networking (IBN) completely changes this scenario by letting the operators set forth the main goals—like ensuring the quality of service or reducing the power consumption—that the system will then follow as a rule to carry out its interventions.

These systems rely on a mix of AI analytics and closed-loop control to constantly make decisions that are in line with the operator's intention. To illustrate, in case there is a sudden increase in network traffic in a certain area, the system can instantly transfer the resources to that area to keep up the performance and this can be done without the need for a manual intervention. Tupl's solutions are the ones that can handle such quick responses, hence, are the building blocks on which self-optimizing, adaptive networks stand.

IBN makes it possible for the network behavior to be guided by the goals rather than the tasks, thus making the policy management more straightforward and fortifying the network. Reducing the reliance on detailed manual configuration allows telecom companies to grow more effectively and, at the same time, to direct their resources toward innovation.

2. **Explainable AI: Building Trust in Automated Decisions**

One of the frequent difficulties in automating telecom processes is attributed to the "black box" feature of numerous AI models that just lead to the output without revealing their reasoning. This lack of clarity leads to reluctance among the engineers who need to check, rely on, and polish those models.

XAI (Explainable AI) resolves this issue by shedding light on the rationale of automatic actions. TuplOS integrates XAI features capable of showing the elements affecting AI choices, facilitating the auditing of results and the taking of actions by network engineers. Efficiency while doing so also guarantees that conventional AI systems conform to industry operational know- how and business requirements.

Telecommunications businesses can increase the AIs' use, make the process of solving problems more efficient and also maintain the supervision of the automation processes if the explainability is there. The ability to alter and retrain the AIs based on the transparent feedback loops of the system is one of the reasons that will make the system reliable and adaptable for a long time.

3. **Closed-Loop Automation: Real-Time Self-Adjustment**

Closed-loop automation is when a system continuously monitors the network status, identifies deviations from the expected performance, and performs the necessary adjustments—all of this is done simultaneously and without involving any human operators. The existence of this characteristic is a must in order to reach the maximum level of automation.

Tupl's cutting-edge technologies, which include the analysis of real-time performance data, the use of historical patterns' learning, and the implementation of AI algorithms, will enable the identification of upcoming problems even before they become serious. To illustrate, in case of detection of low network traffic, the system would immediately reduce energy consumption by disabling energy-saving features proper to that situation thus still ensuring good user experience.

This proactive mode of operation not only improves reliability but also reduces downtime, operational costs, and the burden on human operators. Furthermore, when combined with explainable AI and intent-based networking, closed-loop systems become more intelligent, flexible, and trustworthy.

5.6.2 Top Six Telecom Trends

In the changing scenario, the major factor that would determine the success is the capability of the telco firms to move into digital multi-service platforms and at the same time accept intelligent, open, and self-managed network architectures. Automation, data analytics, and adaptive network technologies are the best practices to follow for the operators to be able to raise their operational efficiency, new services, and competition to a greater extent. The trends that will be telecom industry of the future are discussed in the ensuing paragraphs.

1. **AI-Native and Agentic AI Networks Become the Operating System of Telecom**

In order to provide autonomous optimization, predictive maintenance, and intelligent orchestration across RAN, core, and cloud layers, telecom operators are moving toward AI-native and agentic architectures. With investments shifting from NOC automation to closed-loop RAN/core optimization, agentic provisioning, autonomous slicing, self-healing networks, and AI-governed security, the worldwide AI-in-telecom market is expected to develop at a 38% CAGR through 20301. Benefits include up to 40% fewer call center encounters, 20–25% OPEX savings, and a 30–50% decrease in MTTR. AI-ready workflows and multi-tenant orchestration for independent service delivery are supported by platforms like Smart, while Airtel employs agentic AI for process automation and real-time optimization.

2. **6G Roadmaps Begin to Shape Investments**

worldwide 6G infrastructure expenditure is predicted to surpass $100 billion by the early 2030s5, marking the transition from research to formal worldwide roadmaps. Operators must get ready for new spectrum bands, AI-integrated architectures, sensing-enabled networks, and terahertz communication as commercial momentum picks up around 2026.

Early spectrum planning and cloud-native core improvements are necessary for 6G networks, which are anticipated to provide <1 ms latency, native AI processing, and high-bandwidth sensing applications. By aligning cloud and edge foundations, operators may reduce 6G migration expenses by 20–30%7 by modernizing their 5G SA and edge infrastructure. Telefónica's 6 GHz experiments with UPV and Nokia demonstrate how early network growth is being shaped by mid-band spectrum validation.

3. Open RAN & Network Disaggregation Enter Commercial Scale

As operators look for modular, programmable, and vendor-agnostic networks, open RAN and cloud-native cores are becoming more widely used. The Open RAN market is expected to experience a substantial increase in growth with a whopping 39.4% CAGR at the helm of total cost of ownerships (TCO) being reduced, vendor diversification, and hyperscale collaboration. Standardized, disaggregated RUs can lead to deployment cost reductions of up to 30%, while public macrocells are already contributing more than fifty per cent of the total revenue. Private networks are the segment with the highest growth rate of 34.6% CAGR, and Asia-Pacific is at the forefront of adoption with a 40.7% market share. AT&T's $14B, five-year Open RAN program with Ericsson, which is aimed at having 70% of traffic on open platforms by 2026, does not only signal but also accelerates the commercial scale.

4. Satellite & NTN Connectivity Become Mainstream

NTNs or Non-Terrestrial Networks have started playing a major role in the strategy of 5G and 6G as the alternative communications that include satellites, HAPS, and stratospheric layers get incorporated into the general framework. The market of satellite communication is growing at the rate of 10.2% per annum. NTNs are the ones that make it possible to reach even the most difficult to access places without investing in proportionate RAN CAPEX, thus, making it possible to establish connectivity to remote, maritime, and underserved areas. Direct-to-Device (D2D) services are growing from $0.57B (2025) to $2.64B (2030) at 35.6% CAGR, with 30M IoT connections expected by 2030. The initial commercial milestones like the Eutelsat/MediaTek/Airbus teamwork for the first NTN 5G connection and Starlink's connections with Veon for direct-to-cell service have shown that the industry is ready for new revenue models based on wholesale, roaming, and enterprises. Among operators, satellite backhaul, hybrid terrestrial-satellite plans, NTN-ready devices, and enterprise-grade D2D offerings are the main focus.

5. Telcos Shift to Digital Ecosystem and Value Platforms

The decrease of connectivity as a commodity and the decline in ARPU (mobile at –1.3% CAGR, fixed voice at –4.7% through 2028) is leading the operators to change their business models in favor of digital ecosystem models embracing cloud, IoT, security, fintech, and enterprise platforms. Adjacent digital companies beat conventional telecom revenue, as shown by high-growth operators. IoT, cloud, and security produce €8B1 for Vodafone Business each year, while Singtel's IoT and digital services counteract traditional reductions. Choosing two to three adjacent domains, developing IoT, cloud, and ICT skills, exposing APIs through NaaS/marketplaces, and expanding specialized B2B units are among the investment goals. By facilitating multi-tenant partner onboarding, packaged lifecycle orchestration, and the monetization of connection plus digital services, Smart enables this transformation.

6. **Digital-First Customer Experience Reinvented by eSIM + AI**

As consumers want quick onboarding, seamless roaming, and intelligent assistance, digital-first experiences are increasingly essential to operator differentiation. As the AI-in-telecom market grows from $1.89 billion in 2024 to $50 billion or more by 2034, AI-driven CX is expanding. Up to 95%16 of encounters are handled by AI assistants, increasing accuracy and cutting expenses. While Airtel and other companies use agentic AI for onboarding, upselling, and troubleshooting, Verizon's Gemini-powered assistant handles complicated billing and account issues with >90% accuracy. Through totally digital onboarding, eSIM-first models enable carriers and MVNOs to save acquisition costs, decrease physical distribution, and grow globally. With travel eSIMs increasing from 70 million in 2024 to 280 million in 2030, the worldwide eSIM market is expected to reach $21.75 billion by 2030 (12.85% CAGR). By streamlining device lifecycle management, remote workforce connection, and IoT deployments across markets without complicated SIM logistics, digital-first and eSIM-enabled models help operators.

5.6.3 Key Aspects of Autonomous Network Evolution

- **Intent-Based Networking: Driving Proactive Optimization**

Traditional network operations are primarily reactive, requiring human operators to respond to alarms, investigate issues, and implement fixes. Intent-based networking (IBN) transforms this model by allowing operators to define high-level objectives—such as maintaining quality of service or minimizing energy use—which the system then uses to govern its actions.

These systems leverage a combination of AI analytics and closed-loop control to make real-time decisions aligned with the operator's intent. For instance, if network traffic surges in a particular region, the system can dynamically reallocate resources to maintain performance without manual intervention. Tupl's solutions support such responsiveness, providing the foundation for self-optimizing, adaptive networks.

IBN enables network behavior to be goal-driven rather than task-driven, which simplifies policy management and enhances network resilience. By reducing the need for granular manual configuration, telcos can scale more efficiently and focus resources on innovation.

- **Explainable AI: Building Trust in Automated Decisions**

A common challenge in telecom automation is the "black box" nature of many AI models, which produce results without offering visibility into their decision-making processes. This opacity creates hesitation among engineers who need to validate, trust, and refine those models.

Explainable AI (XAI) addresses this gap by illuminating the reasoning behind automated actions. TuplOS incorporates XAI capabilities that display the factors influencing AI decisions, making it easier for network engineers to audit outcomes and intervene when necessary. This enhances collaboration between human and machine, and ensures AI systems align with operational expertise and business expectations.

With explainability in place, telcos can accelerate AI adoption, streamline troubleshooting, and maintain control over automation deployments. The ability to adjust and retrain AI models based on transparent feedback loops supports long-term system reliability and adaptability.

- **Closed-Loop Automation: Real-Time Self-Adjustment**

Closed-loop automation refers to a system that continuously monitors network conditions, identifies deviations from expected behavior, and implements corrective measures—all in real time and without human input. This capability is foundational to reaching higher levels of automation.

By ingesting real-time performance data, learning from historical patterns, and applying AI algorithms, Tupl solutions can detect emerging issues before they escalate. For example, if network traffic is detected to be low, the engine automatically adjusts energy saving features to optimize energy use without compromising user experience.

This proactive mode of operation not only improves reliability but also reduces downtime, operational costs, and the burden on human operators. Furthermore, when combined with explainable AI and intent-based networking, closed-loop systems become more intelligent, flexible, and trustworthy.

5.6.4 Tupl Solutions Enabling the Automation Journey

Tupl provides a suite of AI-powered tools that help telcos progress across the TM Forum autonomy levels. These tools empower operators to shift from reactive, manual tasks to proactive, strategic operations driven by AI and data insights.

- **TuplOS**: TuplOS acts as the central automation engine, unifying network and IT systems to enable seamless data flow, automation orchestration, and decision-making. It integrates smoothly with operators' systems and processes, such as existing ticketing systems, providing the backbone for scalable automation.
- **Network Advisor**: An AI-based assistant that interprets vast volumes of network data to generate strategic business insights. It automates time-consuming diagnostics and recommends actions based on smart prioritization, helping engineering teams to focus on the most relevant issues to enhance both efficiency and precision in the network troubleshooting processes.
- **NOC Automation**: This solution streamlines operations in NOCs by introducing intelligent protocols that can detect, diagnose, and resolve incidents. It relieves operators of routine monitoring tasks and enables a focus on higher-value activities.
- **Power Saving Advisor**: Power Saving Advisor is a good example of an autonomous operation approach, as it uses AI to assess power usage across network infrastructure and recommend optimization strategies without the need for human intervention. This not only reduces energy consumption but also aligns with corporate environmental goals.

Together, these solutions provide a practical framework for moving from basic automation toward autonomous, self-optimizing networks. They also enable alignment between operational performance and broader business objectives.

5.7 Chapter Summary

The present chapter explored the main points of security, deployment strategies, and directions for future research in contemporary and self-governing telecom networks. It started with a discussion of the changing security situation, drawing attention to the risks that were made worse by the mentioned network technologies that were software-defined, cloud-native, and AI-enabled. Notable security worries, including data confidentiality, model trustworthiness, automation risks, and sophisticated cyber threats, were brought up, highlighting the need for a security system with the ability to adapt, be strong, and be driven by intelligence.

The chapter examined the different deployment models such as centralized, distributed, cloud-based and hybrid architecture and its advantages and disadvantages were compared to scalability, performance and operational efficiency. One of the ways stated to ensure interoperability, vendor neutrality and flexibility in multi-vendor environments was a necessity of standardization and opening up of network architectures. Further, the introduction of resilience, fault tolerance, and reliability strategies as the basic design principles to ensure that service interruption will never occur and that the effect of network disruption will become minimal possible was done in quite a positive and optimistic manner.

The discussion in the chapter eventually contributed to the discovery of the areas that the telecommunication networks would explore in the near future with the focus put on the AI-powered networking, automatic recovery system, user-intent-driven networking, and the latest wireless technologies. Ensuring a scenario, in which telecom networks are characterized by a higher level of independence, smartness, and flexibility, the envisioned breakthroughs are described.

Very Short Questions

1. Term for networks continuing despite failures?
2. What protocol is standardized for internet communication?
3. What model combines on-premises and cloud resources?
4. Which cloud model reduces vendor lock-in?
5. Name one public cloud provider.
6. What technology is expected in 6G for <1 ms latency?
7. What does ORAN focus on?
8. What does AI stand for in telecom networks?
9. Name one benefit of feature flags.
10. What is XAI short for?

Short Questions

1. How do feature flags help reduce deployment risks?
2. Why is network standardization important for 5G?
3. Explain the main difference between private and public cloud deployment.
4. Give an example of a use case for hybrid cloud deployment.
5. How does closed-loop automation improve network operations?
6. What role does intent-based networking play in AI automation?
7. Name two security risks associated with AI in telecom networks.
8. What does fault tolerance ensure in distributed systems?
9. Why is explainable AI important for telecom engineers?
10. What is the key benefit of a multicloud environment?

MCQs (Multiple Choice Questions)

1. **Which deployment model offers infrastructure solely for one organization?**
   A. Public Cloud
   B. Private Cloud
   C. Hybrid Cloud
   D. Multicloud
2. **Feature flags primarily help with:**
   A. Network disaggregation

B. Gradual rollout of new features

C. Hardware provisioning

D. Spectrum allocation

3. **Intent-based networking focuses on:**

A. Human-operated troubleshooting

B. Automatic decision-making guided by goals

C. Manual feature flag deployment

D. Satellite network setup

4. **Which cloud model reduces the chance of service downtime using multiple providers?**

A. Public Cloud

B. Private Cloud

C. Hybrid Cloud

D. Multicloud

5. **Closed-loop automation is best described as:**

A. A manual troubleshooting method

B. Real-time system self-adjustments

C. Vendor lock-in strategy

D. Standard protocol creation

6. **One of the security risks in AI-enabled telecom networks is:**

A. Overprovisioning

B. Algorithmic bias

C. Faster deployment

D. Multicloud flexibility

7. **Which of the following is a public cloud provider?**

A. Microsoft Azure

B. Private Data Center

C. Hybrid Cloud

D. Edge Node

8. **What is the purpose of network standardization?**

A. Reduce infrastructure costs only

B. Ensure interoperability and consistency

C. Increase cloud vendor lock-in

D. Replace all hardware

9. Which protocol is a standardized rule for network communication?

A. HTTP

B. SQL

C. FTP

D. SMTP

10. What is a main challenge of hybrid cloud?

A. Scalability

B. Management complexity

C. Vendor lock-in

D. High latency

MCQ Answer sheet

Q1	Q2	Q3	Q4	Q5	Q6	Q7	Q8	Q9	Q10
B	B	B	B	B	B	A	B	A	B

Chapter 6: Intent-Driven Telecom Networks and Provisioning

6.1 Chapter Introduction

Due to the changing nature of the telecom industry (as the industry transitions into 5G-Advanced and 6G), operators face the challenges of changing customer demand, changing network complexity, proliferating enterprise and ecosystem use cases (B2C, B2B2X, IoT), and unequalled technological advancement across the network, cloud, and AI domains.

These changes radically transform value-generation and capture models - new models of monetization and reshaped BSS are required to remain competitive and relevant.

The operational backbone of operators is Business Support Systems (BSS) that operate the products, orders, revenue (charging and billing) and customer relationships. Being the main point of almost all customer contacts, the success and effectiveness of BSS directly influences the quality of customer experience and the effectiveness of the digital provision of services.

Traditional traffic-based revenue models are no longer sufficient. Coming into focus is experience-based monetization, where value is measured and charged based on the quality, reliability, and outcomes delivered to end users and

ecosystem partners. This necessitates the development of BSS platforms beyond the rule-based fixed systems to be dynamic intelligent engines which are capable of supporting real-time charging, flexible pricing and personalization of services to various segments of the market.

This transformation can be brought about by intent-driven autonomous networks. One can be able to automate service lifecycle management, simplify operational complexity and optimize performance depending on real-time conditions and user experience by aligning network behavior to business intent.

This change is being facilitated by standardization organizations like 3GPP, TM Forum, and O-RAN Alliance using open, programmable architectures and APIs.

Decision making autonomy, adaptability and learning of system with minimal human intervention or none at all is being propelled by emerging agentic AI architectures and design patterns. These are the basis of autonomous networks.

An example is that TM Forum defines intent as, the formal description of the entire expectations such as requirements, goals, to a technical system as constraints.

This paper has examined concepts that can be used by the operators in order to take advantage of intent-driven operations at both network and BSS layers. One result of this notion is varied connectivity which can open new sources of revenue with agility, personalization, simplicity and automation being the foundational basis of digital service models in the future.

This whitepaper offers ideas to shift to autonomous operations rather than manual and automated operations in the BSS field.

6.2 Understanding Intent

From Autonomous Network to Business Function

Customers in the modern diverse and rapidly changing environment include cost-effective individuals as well as those with high enterprises.

reliability and privacy needs, expect individual service experiences. Meanwhile, operators are interested in pursuing profitability, security, cost reduction, and regulatory compliance. The operations that are intent motivated and can be autonomously controlled by having closed control loops assist to create the environment of scalable, intelligent, and adaptive networks.

The operational support of operators is Business Support Systems (BSS) which deals with products, orders, revenue (charging and billing), and customer relationships. Being the main point of interaction with almost all the customers, the quality of customer experience and the effectiveness of online service delivery is directly dependent on the performance and agility of BSS.

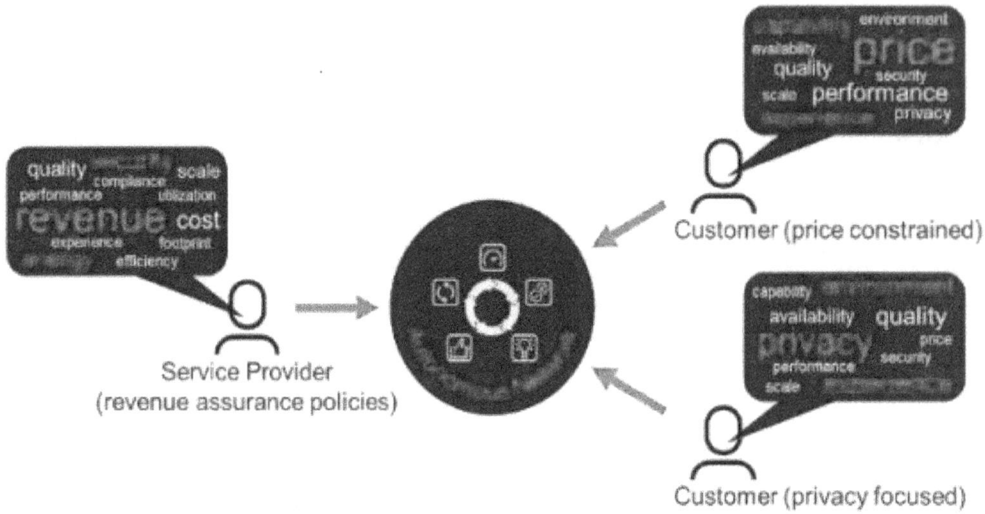

Figure 6.1: Interested parties of an autonomous network

Source: (Niemöller, 2022)

6.2.1 What is Intent

Intent is the expression of requirements from any stakeholder—be it a customer or a CSP.

It defines what needs to be achieved, and not how to do it. This allows networks to act autonomously within defined parameters, translating business goals into operational outcomes without prescribed step-by-step instructions.

Intent can be expressed in both human-readable and machine-readable formats. Standards like 3GPP and TM Forum have defined models and ontologies to formalize this. Standardization has created various information models for expressing and managing intent. For example, 3GPP defines intent expression models for RAN operation. TM Forum has proposed the TM Forum intent ontology which, in combination with TM Forum Open APIs, primarily targets the use of intent in product and service management.

To realize intent and capture it from the customer / user and the whole way to the resources, a layered cognitive network architecture, broken down into Business, Services and Resources, is proposed. In each layer, one or more intent managers are responsible for handling all intents given and take the right actions to fulfil the intents.

The roles of BSS and OSS network domains span across all the three layers of Business, Service and Resource.

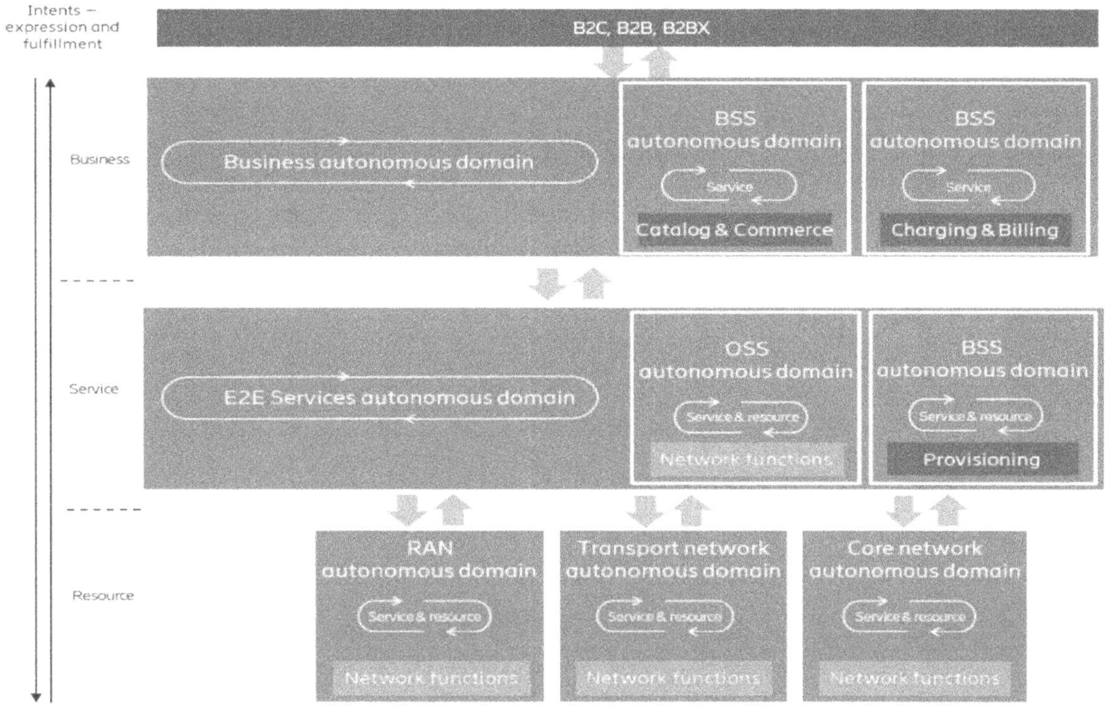

Figure 6.2: The cognitive network with several layers, all interacting through intents.

Source: (Niemöller, 2022)

6.2.2 Intent Management

In the architecture of an intent-based cognitive network, the intent management function coordinates the autonomous operation to meet the objectives and requirements stated by intent.

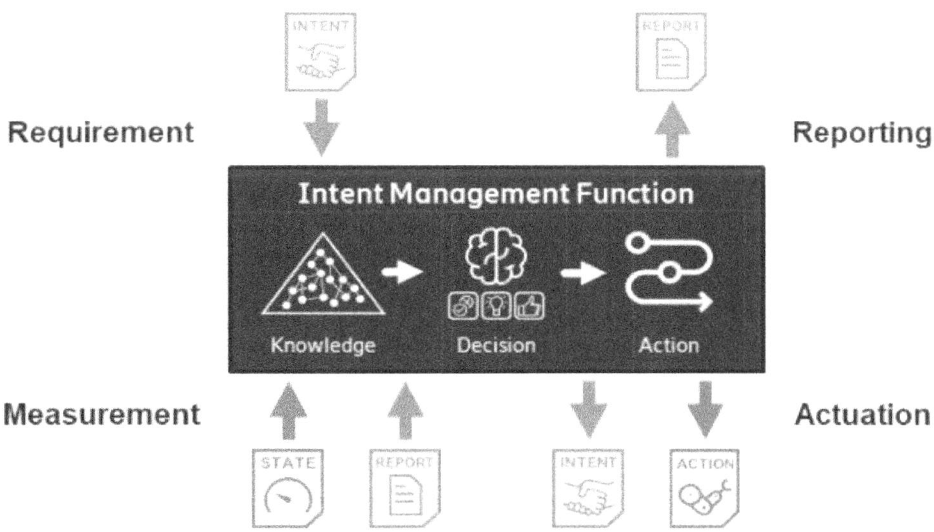

Figure 6.3: Intent Management Function

Source: (Niemöller, 2022)

An intent management function (IMF) receives intents that constitute knowledge about the requirements an intent management function is asked to fulfill.

The important point is that every detailed requirement defined in the intent is measurable. This allows the intent management function to continuously monitor if it meets its requirements and act if not.

Using Advance AI, IMFs enhance capabilities like prediction, anomaly detection, and optimization. Generative AI enable intuitive interactions and adaptive decision-making, even under new or complex conditions.

For every intent it has received, an intent management function is sending reports back to the originator of the intent to keep it informed about fulfillment status. Humans can be in the loop as and when they desire to be part of the loop. This forms a control loop between two instances of the intent management function. One has sent the intent to define requirements. This intent management function is referred to as intent owner. The other has received the intent and operates according to the requirements within. This intent management function is referred to as intent handler.

An intent management function has the capability to decide on actions and action strategies for improving intent fulfilment.

After a decision was made to act, the intent handling function will initiate actuation. It can utilize conventional interfaces that allow, for example, the change of resource configuration or the initiation of processes and services. Another way to act would be the creation of one or more further intents.

6.2.3 Closed control loops with Intent Management Functions

Closed control loops in IMF detect deviations, analyze causes, and take corrective actions—such as reconfiguring the network or delegating tasks to other IMFs.

Intent management functions are typically realized as a closed continuous control loop. They observe through measurement if all requirements are met or through prediction if the system is in danger of not meeting requirements anymore. This allows them to identify potential issues and start acting to solve them.

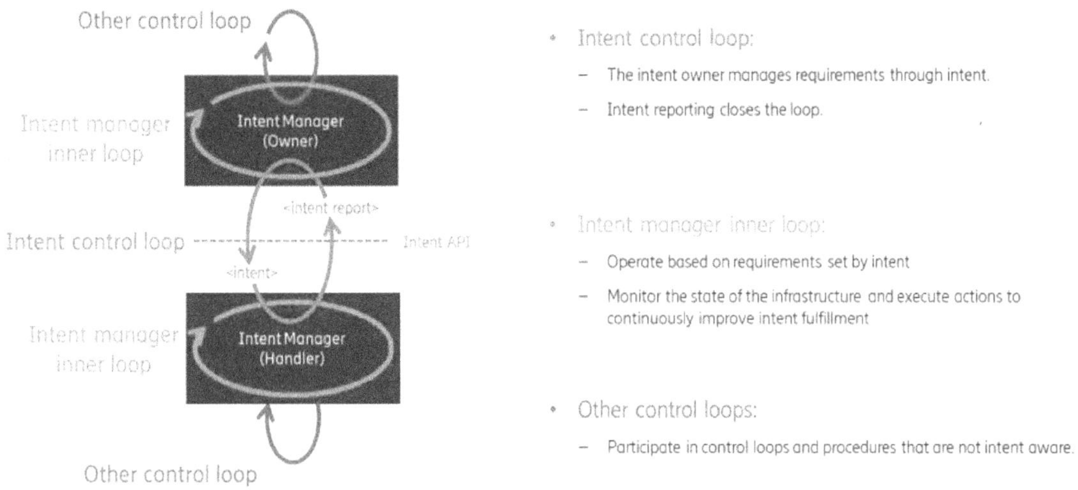

Figure 6.4: Control loops in intent-based operation

Source: (Niemöller, 2022)

6.2.4 Architecture Principles

The architectural principles guide the design of the system capabilities required to achieve the desired autonomy levels within autonomous domains and autonomous networks.

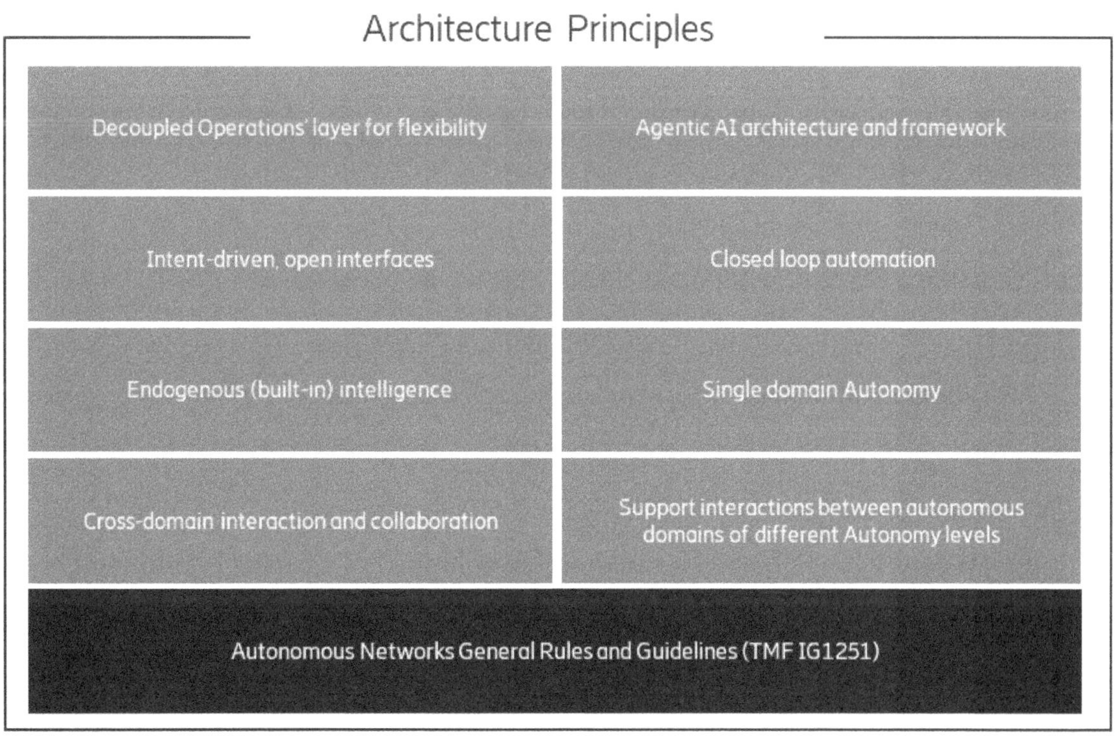

Figure 6.5: Architectural Principles

Source: (Niemöller, 2022)

As covered in the above figure, core architectural principles guide the design of the capabilities required to achieve the desired autonomy levels with autonomous domains and autonomous networks:

- **Decoupled Operations layers for operational flexibility:** The network is divided into three independent layers—business, service, and resource—each working on its own and hiding internal details, making the system more flexible and easier to manage.
- **Intent-driven, open interfaces:** Each part of the network should use standard, open interfaces—ideally intent-based—so higher layers can easily communicate what they want without needing to know the technical details.
- **Closed loop automation:** The system uses a smart feedback loop to monitor, analyze, and adjust itself automatically keeping everything running smoothly without needing human help.
- **Endogenous (Built-In) Intelligence:** The network uses built-in, local intelligence—like AI and real-time insights—to understand and act on its environment, making faster and smarter decisions close to where data is generated.
- **Agentic AI architecture and framework:** Agents that are self-reliant, can make decisions on their own and with no or little help from humans. Acting on real time data or near real time data for decision-making enhances autonomy within the domains.
- **Single Domain Autonomy:** There is independence in each component of the network as it is a building block of self-contained intelligence and control, and it is less complicated to control and scale the entire system compared to putting together Lego pieces.
- **Cross Domain Collaboration:** Even though each domain works on its own, they must still work together to deliver full services, share goals, and coordinate tasks—like a team where each player knows their role but also supports the others.
- **Supports interactions between autonomous domains of different Autonomy Levels:** Domains with different levels of automation should be able to work together, and each domain can grow or adapt its autonomy level over time based on its capabilities and changing needs.

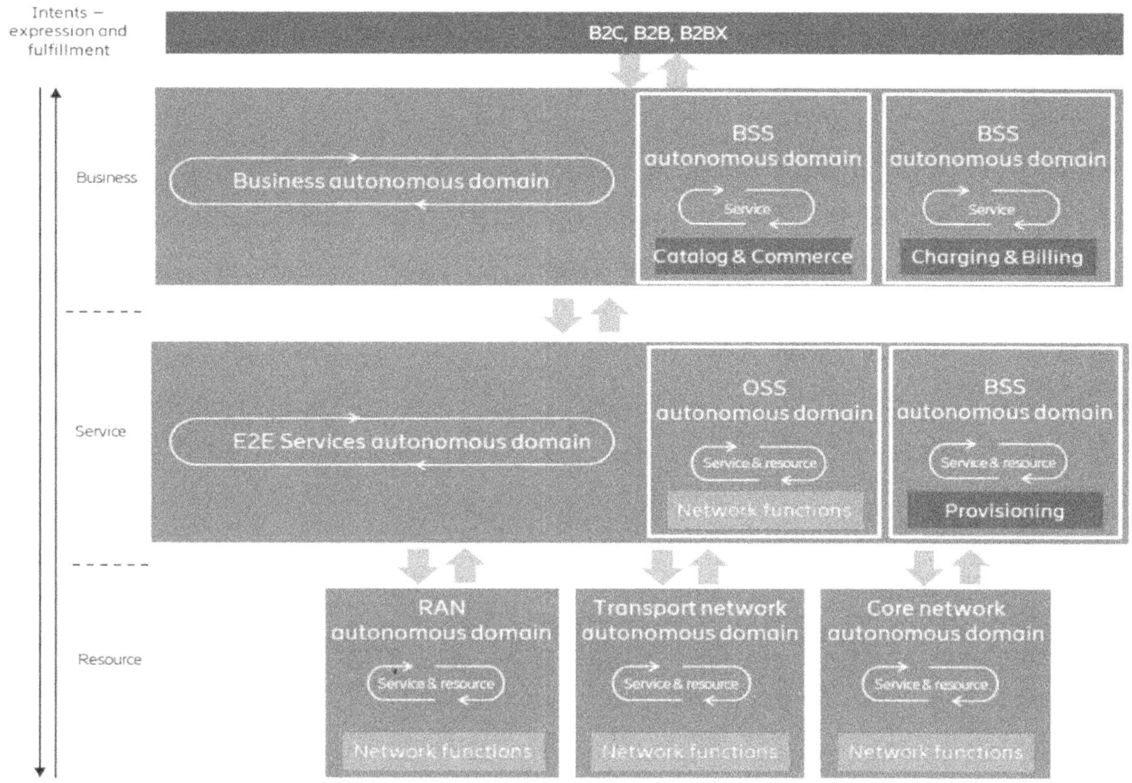

Figure 6.6: Autonomous n/w enablement covering business, service, and resource operation layer.

Source: (Niemöller, 2022)

6.3 Intent-Driven Networks

As a foundation to monetize differentiated connectivity services, Intent-driven autonomous networks enable Next-Gen BSS to dynamically align service delivery with customer intent. It also optimizes resource utilization in real time, and supports new agile monetization models required for 5G, network slicing, and enterprise-grade SLAs.

In a recent report on differentiated 5G connectivity, the monetization potential of 5G standalone (SA) was analyzed. Differentiated connectivity services beyond best-effort mobile broadband are anticipated to enable increased revenue growth and profitability, providing new value for operators.

An autonomous network is subdivided into autonomous domains according to the generic architecture proposed by TM Forum. According to this generic architecture, autonomous domains have a specific responsibility scope within the overall autonomous network. Autonomous domains also interact by setting requirements using intent.

Based on the Autonomous Network reference architecture defined by TM Forum, Network operation within an autonomous network may be described with three layers: business operations, service operations and resource operations. The functions within these layers and autonomous domains interact through open and standardized

interfaces. TM Forum has published the TMF921 API for general purpose intent management between intent owners and intent handlers, enabling operations such as providing intents, reporting on compliance status, modifying requirements and removing intents.

TM Forum also introduces intent management capabilities into the APIs used in product and service management. TMF620, TMF633 and TMF634 as well as into ordering APIs such as TMF622 and TMF641 include examples hereof. These evolved APIs allow managing and ordering products and service while managing the related product and service intent that expresses detailed product and service requirements. Also, Intent feasibility checks can be combined with product and service qualification through the APIs TMF679 and TMF645.

6.3.1 Intent in Business Layer – overview

In the context of intent-driven autonomous networks, the Business Layer serves as the strategic control point where high-level business objectives are defined and initiated. This layer is responsible for capturing business intents— statements of what the organization wants to achieve—without requiring knowledge of how those goals will be

operationally fulfilled.

This abstraction enables greater agility, automation, and alignment between business strategy and network operations, as defined in TM Forum's Open Digital Architecture (ODA) and IG1228: Intent-Based Management Framework.

In TMF's Open Digital Architecture, the Business Layer maps primarily to the following domains:

- **Engagement Management:** Interfaces for customer interaction and intent capture.
- **Core Commerce:** Product, offer, and revenue management (Charging and Billing).
- **Intelligence Management:** Analytics and AI-driven decision support.

These domains interact with the Service Orchestration and Resource Management layers through intent-based APIs, enabling seamless translation of business goals into automated network actions.

The BSS domain intent management spans across all the three layers.

6.3.2 Intent in e2e Service Layer

As it is the heart of network operation, the service management domain is the starting point for the introduction of intents, where intents are a prerequisite for autonomous operation.

The primary purpose of the service-layer intent manager is the realization and assurance of E2E service in accordance with service requirements received from the business layer. Compliance to intent received from the business layer is

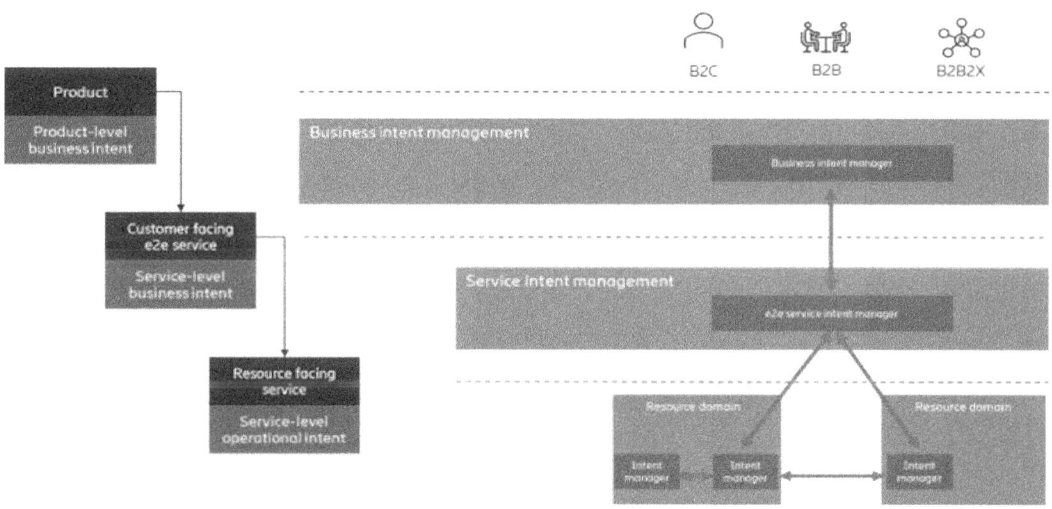

Figure 6.7: Product and Service breakdown in the layered intent management architecture.

Source: (Niemöller, 2022)

the terminal function of the service layer. Central to achieving this function is the translation of service intent into instrumental goals which constitute resource-layer requirements for individual resource domains. The idea is that the business intent is met as long as each individual resource domain remains compliant to its assigned intent.

The intent manager orders the selected services from the orchestrator resulting in various actions toward resource domains. The E2E intent manager also monitors the continued fulfillment of the customer requirements.

The E2E service orchestrator would apply a catalog-driven composition to determine the RFSs to be configured and instantiated and would use the intent-defined requirements to make decisions in provisioning.

6.3.3 Intent in RAN

Specific examples of RAN intents include average downlink and uplink throughputs, packet latencies, geographically aware services, and time of day scheduling. Intents in the RAN resource operations layer enter at the RAN resource Service Management and Orchestration (SMO) level. In an Open RAN SMO-based solution, RAN IMFs may also be realized as rApps, where these RAN intent reports are augmented. These intents are subsequently managed by the RAN IMF which could be an Intent management rApp and, if feasible, be distributed to a lower layer gNode-B. Once mapped, the distributed RAN intent control on gNode-B software functionality adapts to maximize fulfilment of intents on the cell. This includes aspects of system parameters, internal states and variables controlling the number of active connections, user experiences, resource consumption and system loads. As a part of the RAN intent observability on the SMO, and in closing the loop, intent fulfillment is measured on the rApp which adjusts targets on cluster level where required.

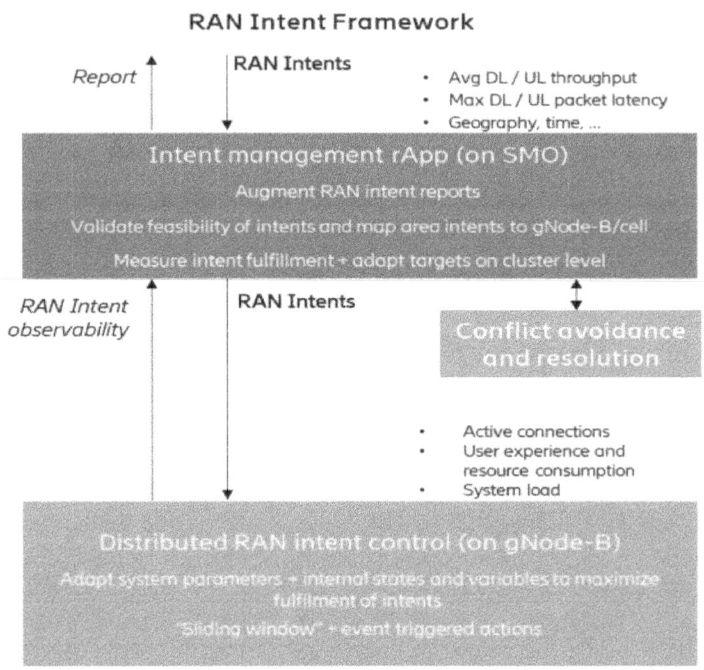

Figure 6.8: Example of possible Intent driven RAN architecture.

Source: (Niemöller, 2022)

Depending on the capabilities of the RAN NFs, the RAN IMF decides whether to process and forward a decomposed intent to the autonomous domain defined by the RAN NF, or to realize the requirements in the intent through traditional configuration of RAN NF features. Forwarding the intent implies that the RAN NF will take actions to assure the intent within its autonomous domain. While the intent handler in the RAN management level may orchestrate multiple radio nodes to assure the RAN service over a larger RAN area (e.g. a cluster of cells), the intent handler in the RAN NF will be responsible for its resources and will be able to take actions related to the associated cell's coverage area.

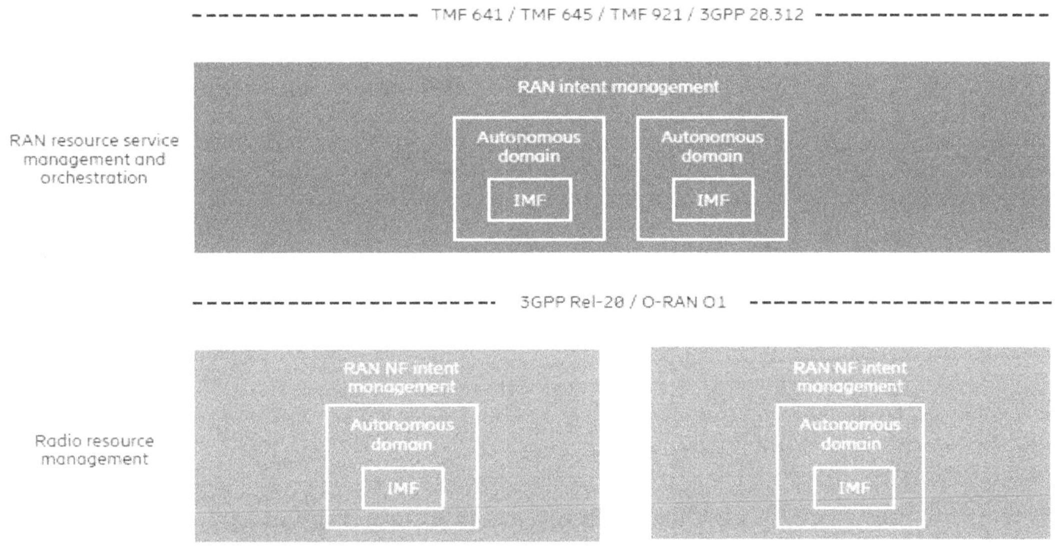

Figure 6.9: Autonomous RAN enablement on the resource operations layer.

Source: (Niemöller, 2022)

6.3.4 What problems does intent-based networking solve?

Traditionally, networking has been driven by manual, command-line interface (CLI)-based operations, basic element management systems (EMSs), or automation scripts. Most network outages result from human errors that occur during these network operations.

Intent-based networking reduces errors and risk while improving operational efficiencies in several ways.

- Validates intent objects before applying them to the network. Intent objects are high-level representations of the desired properties or outcomes to be achieved with the network. Validation is syntactic and includes semantic checks against networkwide policy.

- Instantaneous roll-back or roll-forward. Operators simply apply the appropriate versioned intent object to return to a known good state if something goes wrong during a deployment push.
- Limits the impact and scope of failures during new intent rollout through well-defined policy.
- Intent-based fallback. As the system knows the desired outcomes for a specific configuration, it can maintain those outcomes even in the face of outages or device errors by reconfiguring other network elements or using different mechanisms to achieve the same results.

Modern network orchestration systems have made commercial, intent-based network systems for mission-critical and scaled deployments possible. Intent-based networks dramatically reduce the time to deliver reliable services from days or weeks to minutes and help address operational challenges once the infrastructure has been deployed.

6.3.5 Evolving to intent-based networking

While intent-based networking is not a new concept, most companies are still somewhere on the evolutionary path toward achieving it.

Each stage along the way is characterized by increasingly automated and simpler ways of deploying and managing network operations.

- **Manual**–Operations staff imperatively manage data center network devices using CLI, SNMP, and basic and discrete tools.
- **Semiautomated**–Scripts and rules-based management combine with traditional tools for basic automation, visibility into network data, and alerts that enable reaction to network events.
- **Software**-defined data center–A software abstraction of the network infrastructure enables faster, secure deployment of services and applications.
- **Automation**-centric data center–Builds upon the software-defined data center by automating provisioning, configuration, deployment, and orchestration.

- **Intent-based data center**–Continually collects and converts all pertinent data needed to take the automated actions that keep the network aligned with dynamic business intent, data center conditions, and policies.

6.4 Intent in Business Layer – A Deeper Dive

The central concern of a business support system (BSS) is to help the operators capitalize on the investments it makes in its network infrastructure, partner ecosystem, business models and multi-channel engagements. At the same time, operator also maximizes its profitability and delivers a rich experience for consumers and enterprises. The decisions taken to realize the desired business outcomes can be seen as reasoning under uncertainty. Intent-based management is well suited to operate in this environment and at the same time enhance and simplify.

The transition from legacy BSS to an intent-driven, Next-Gen BSS requires a fundamental architectural evolution—one that embraces cloud-native, microservices-based design, real-time responsiveness, and experience-centric principles.

To achieve the transition to Next-Gen BSS operators should adopt TM Forum's Open Digital Architecture (ODA) and leverage standardized Open APIs. This enables interoperability, agility, and modularity across the ecosystem. These standards provide the blueprint for building modular, composable & intent-aware business capabilities that can dynamically respond to customer needs and network conditions. By aligning with ODA and simplifying the BSS landscape, operators can accelerate innovation, reduce integration complexity, and deliver differentiated, intent-driven services at scale.

Capability Area	Description
Customer & Party Management	Captures customer-driven intents (e.g., service preferences, experience goals)
Intent based provisioning	Intent based subscriber provisioning enabling auto provisioning of users
Dynamic Product Catalog	Enables business users to define product intents
Revenue Management (Next-Gen Charging)	Real-time rating, metering, and deduction of usage-based services as they occur
Revenue Management (Next-Gen	Manages invoicing, account balance management,

Billing)	discounts, and financial reporting
Intent Capture & Translation	Core function for expressing and managing business-level intents
Analytics & Insights	Enables closed-loop feedback to adjust or refine business intents dynamically

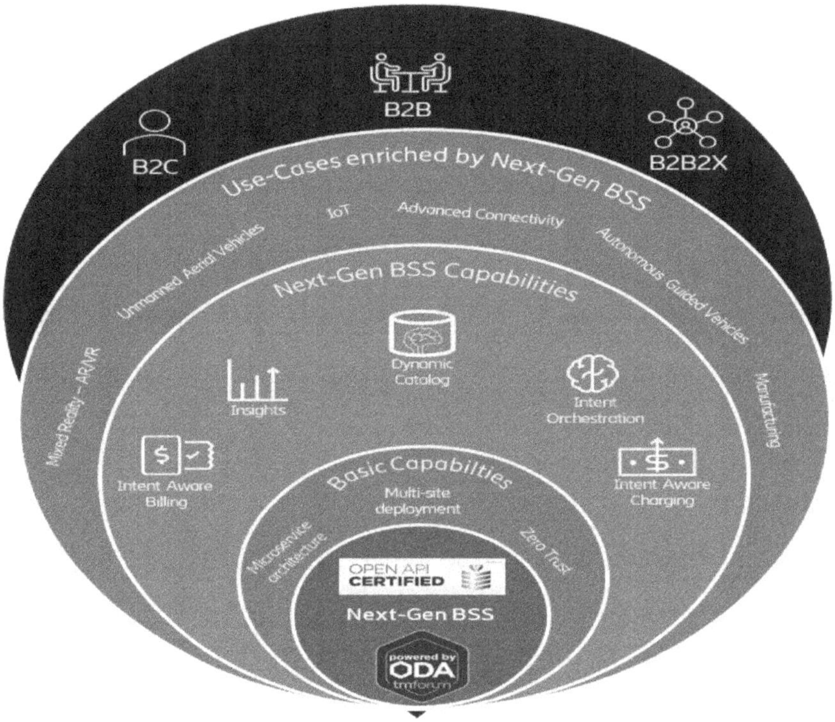

Figure 6.10: Digital eco-system enabled by Next-Gen BSS with intent-based architecture.

Source: (Niemöller, 2022)

The figure above depicts an operator's Eco-System that could leverage a monetization of diverse use cases across consumer and partner segments.

Some key capabilities that shall enable it are listed in the table below:

Achieving an intent-driven architecture requires embedding customer and party management, intent capture & translation, and analytics-driven insights as foundational capabilities that enable operators to understand, interpret, and act on customer expectations.

While these capabilities set the context for intent expression and feedback, in the next section we'll focus on the execution layers—specifically Dynamic Product Catalog, Orchestration, Next-Gen

Charging, and Next-Gen Billing— which operationalize intent through agile offer design, real-time usage monetization, and flexible revenue

management.

Let us start with some sample use cases to set the monetization context.

6.4.1 Intent Driven Monetization – Sample use cases

By aligning to the necessary architecture, needed functions and capabilities for future business layers can be both derived and realized by looking into some of the uses cases listed below.

Table 6.1: Sample use cases for Intent Driven Monetization

Use Case	Description	Technical Requirements	Monetization Model	Role of Intent
Immersive AR/VR Experiences	Live 4K VR concert streaming with seamless, high-quality delivery.	High-bandwidth, low-latency sessions; Edge GPU compute; Network slicing.	Pay-per-minute pricing; Tiered quality levels (HD, 4K, holographic).	Defines QoE parameters; Enables dynamic resource allocation and real-time prioritization.
Autonomous Drone Delivery	Drone delivery services requiring ultra-reliable low-latency communication and real-time telemetry.	URLLC; Access to telemetry and airspace data; Edge-hosted applications.	Composite charging based on duration, distance, API usage, and prioritization.	Specifies start and end points, delivery time windows, and reliability requirements; Translates into composite service intents.
Remote Robotic Healthcare	Robotic surgery with bi-directional ultra-low latency and	Real-time, secure, low-latency communication; Encrypted data channels; SLA-	Session-based charging; SLA and privacy-grade–based pricing.	Captures criticality and sensitivity of the service; Ensures network provisions resources that meet stringent

	haptic feedback, requiring strict security and privacy.	backed service assurance.		thresholds.
Smart City Congestion Pricing	Dynamic congestion pricing supported by real-time traffic analytics and networked cameras.	Guaranteed bandwidth for traffic analytics; Dynamic prioritization during congestion.	API call–based charging; Surge pricing based on congestion levels.	Expresses need for dynamic prioritization of traffic management services; Enables adaptive resource allocation and policy enforcement.
Intent-Based IoT Monetization	Spot pricing models utilizing unused network capacity for IoT devices with flexible communication windows.	Dynamic pricing engine; Real-time network utilization monitoring.	Spot pricing based on network load; Targeted offers for specific IoT segments.	Defines pricing strategies, target segments, and utilization thresholds; Influences decision- making logic of the business layer.

6.4.2 Intent based provisioning

In intent-driven autonomous networks, subscriber provisioning is very critical to the autonomous functioning of the

networks. Subscriber provisioning is very critical to the autonomy in the different autonomous domains dependent on the subscriber information. This could be e2e service autonomous domain involving e2e service orchestration and assurance but also the autonomous behavior of charging and billing part of the BSS autonomous domains. Provisioning will act as an important bridge between Core Commerce and Customer Engagement systems in the Business layer and many solutions like Charging and Orchestration providing services in the Services layer.

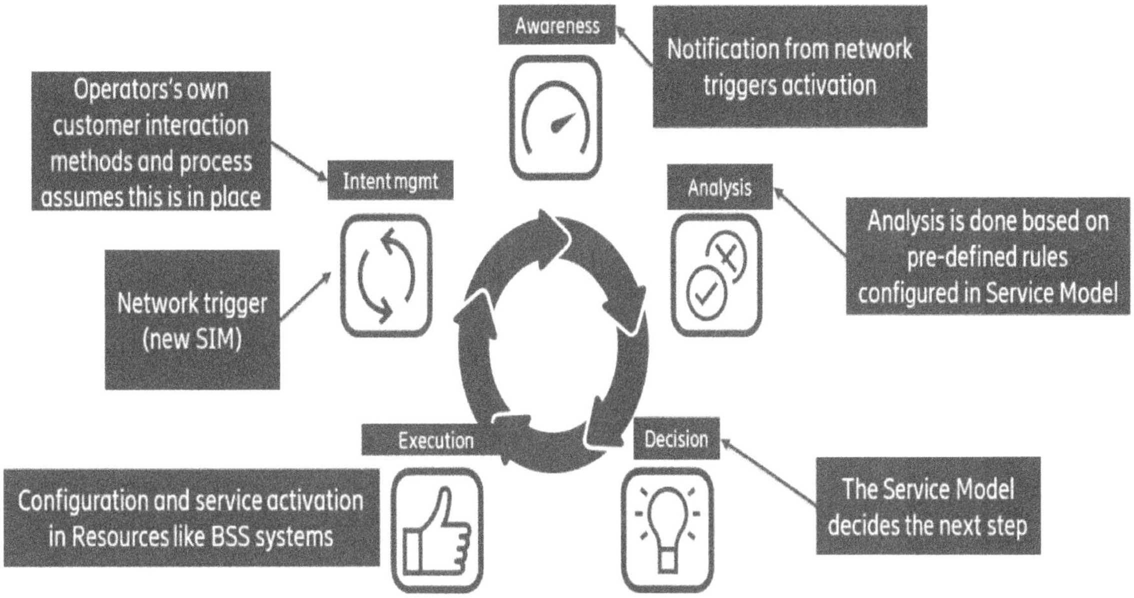

Figure 6.11: An example use-case of intent based provisioning IMF

Source: (Niemöller, 2022)

The intent management function (IMF) of a provisioning system, is acting on the operator / CSP provisioned rules and policies and is expecting a trigger from the network to initiate the auto-provisioning loop. Analysis based on the pre- defined rules leads to decision making. The actuation or execution leads to configuration or service activation in other systems. This closed loop automation is realized through agentic AI framework.

6.4.3 Dynamic Product Catalog – Composing Personalized Services

In intent-driven autonomous networks, customer interaction often begins with a natural language conversation— powered by large language models (LLMs)—where users express what they want to achieve rather than specifying

technical service parameters. The network interprets this intent and dynamically matches it to available or composable products.

At the core of this capability lies the dynamic product catalog—a foundational component that enables real-time creation, adaptation, and lifecycle management of personalized offerings. Unlike static catalogs, dynamic catalogs support:

- On-demand product generation tailored to individual users or segments.
- Real-time modification of active products based on evolving needs.

- Retirement and replacement of offerings as user context changes.

To ensure interoperability and agility, operators must adopt TM Forum's Open APIs—such as TMF620 (Product Catalog), TMF622 (Product Ordering), and TMF679 (Product Offering Qualification). These APIs, aligned with the Open Digital Architecture (ODA), enable modular, standards-based integration between the business and service layers.

Furthermore, intent negotiation between the business and service layers ensures that dynamically composed products are technically feasible before being offered. This includes evaluating service availability, resource costs, and user

experience guarantees. The catalog evolution to Master Catalog is critical to ensure that Business, Service and Resource layers can use the same catalog.

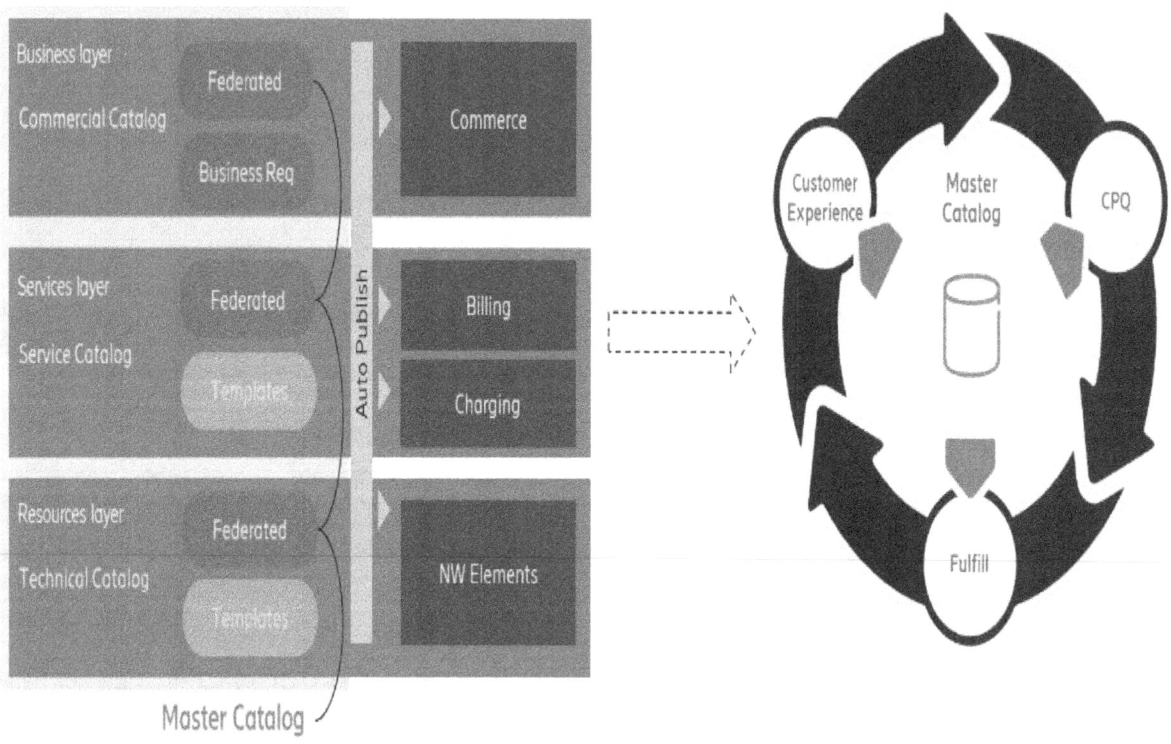

Figure 6.12: Catalog Evolution – Master Catalog for All three Intent layers.

Source: (Niemöller, 2022)

Finally, dynamic catalogs support flexible pricing and charging models that reflect both the operational effort and the customer's business value—enabling operators to deliver personalized, profitable, and scalable digital experiences.

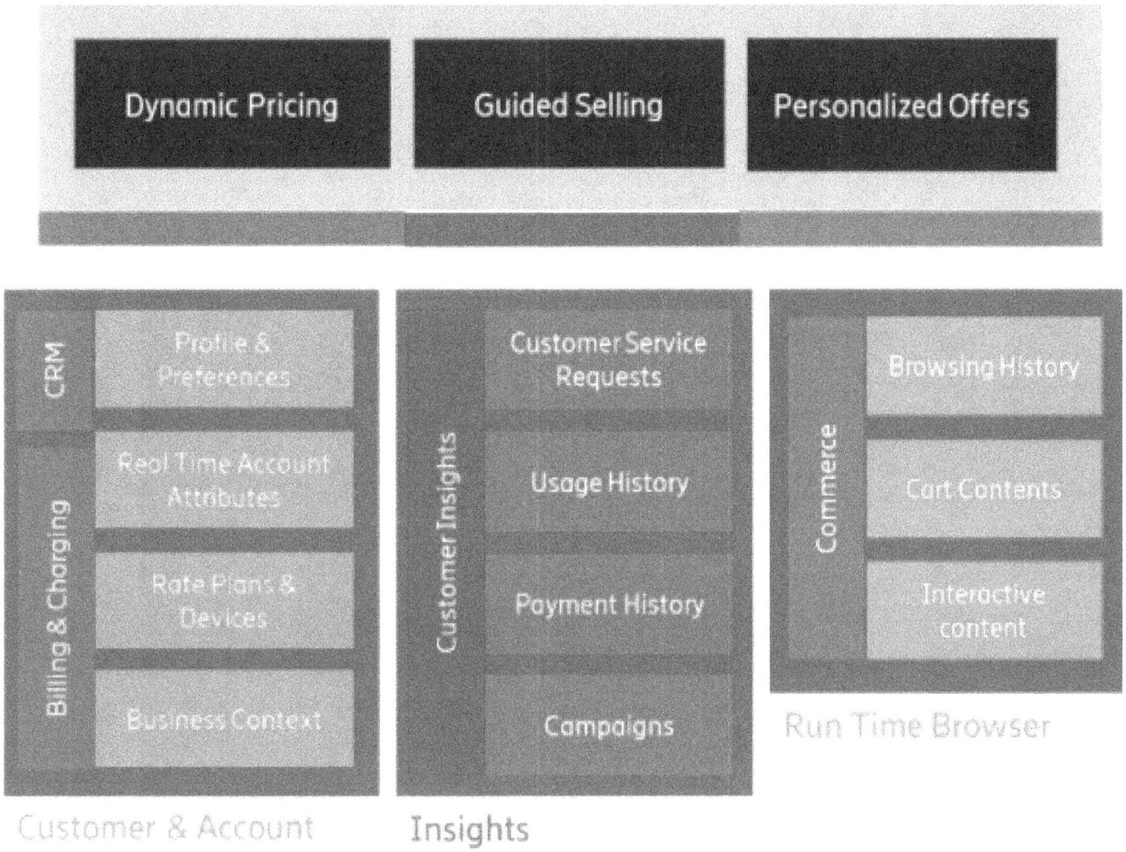

Figure 6.13: Features that a catalog would need to support for intent-based networks.

Source: (Niemöller, 2022)

6.4.4 Intent Orchestration and Assurance

If the offered cart is ordered the respective services are ordered from the service layer and delivery of the product through service fulfilment starts. Intent is used in association with the service order to manage the requirement the intent management of the service layer needs to meet. The intent requirements drive not only the initial fulfilment of the services, but also the continued assurance. In the service layer the intent assurance it therefore realized by service assurance. The intent management function of the service layer is therefore a combination of service orchestration and service assurance.

Intent can also be used to steer the resource usage and network operation below the service layer, but within a well- designed autonomous network the details are transparent for the business layer.

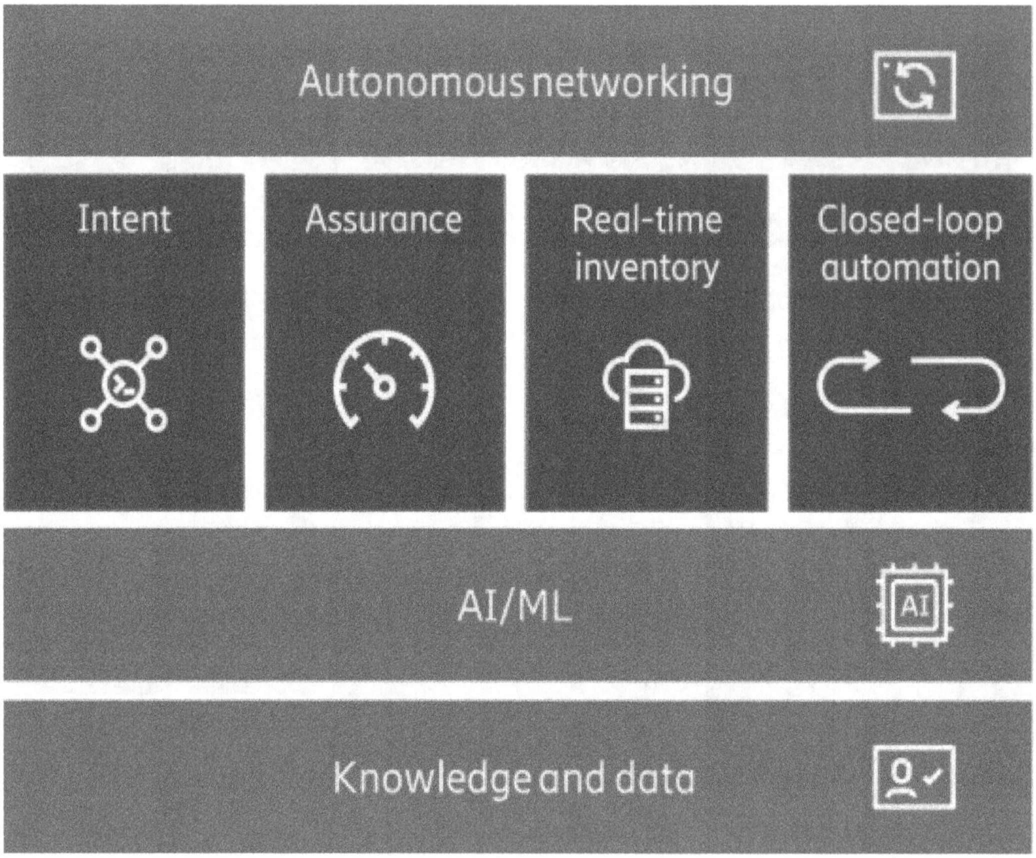

Figure 6.14: Building blocks of an Intent-based service orchestration. Intent orchestration and assurance provide the needed platform to:

Source: (Niemöller, 2022)

- **Enable new services:** through differentiated connectivity and programmability.
- **Manage complexity:** deliver services quickly by transforming to autonomous network.
- **Combine:** intent, assurance, real-time inventory, CLA, agentic AI and knowledge
- **Operate services:** in any environment, multi-domain, multi-vendor, multi-technology.
- **Speed up innovation:** Use an open, standards-based architecture.

6.4.5 Next-Gen Charging and Next-Gen Billing

Legacy BSS needs to evolve to meet the demands of the Next-Gen Networks and services.

Many operators still rely on ofline or batch-based rating/charging engines which are ill-suited for the real-time, usage- based monetization required in 5G and beyond networks. This truly constraints the ability to monetize intent-based or differentiated experience-based services, affecting revenue and service agility.

As covered in the chapter above, apart from dynamic catalog and intent orchestration, Next-Gen Charging and Billing would play a pivotal role in monetizing the new uses cases. Below are some key principles that would drive the Next- Gen architecture:

- **Real-time, SLA-Aware:** Enabling flexible monetization models to respond to real-time network conditions and service-level agreements.
- **Cloud-Native and Microservices Architectures:** Adopting flexible, scalable systems that can be easily updated and integrated with other digital platforms using Open APIs.
- **AI and Automation:** Leveraging AI for predictive analytics, automated decision-making, and enhanced customer experiences.
- **Support for New Monetization Models:** Support new multi-sided business models (B2X/B2B2X)

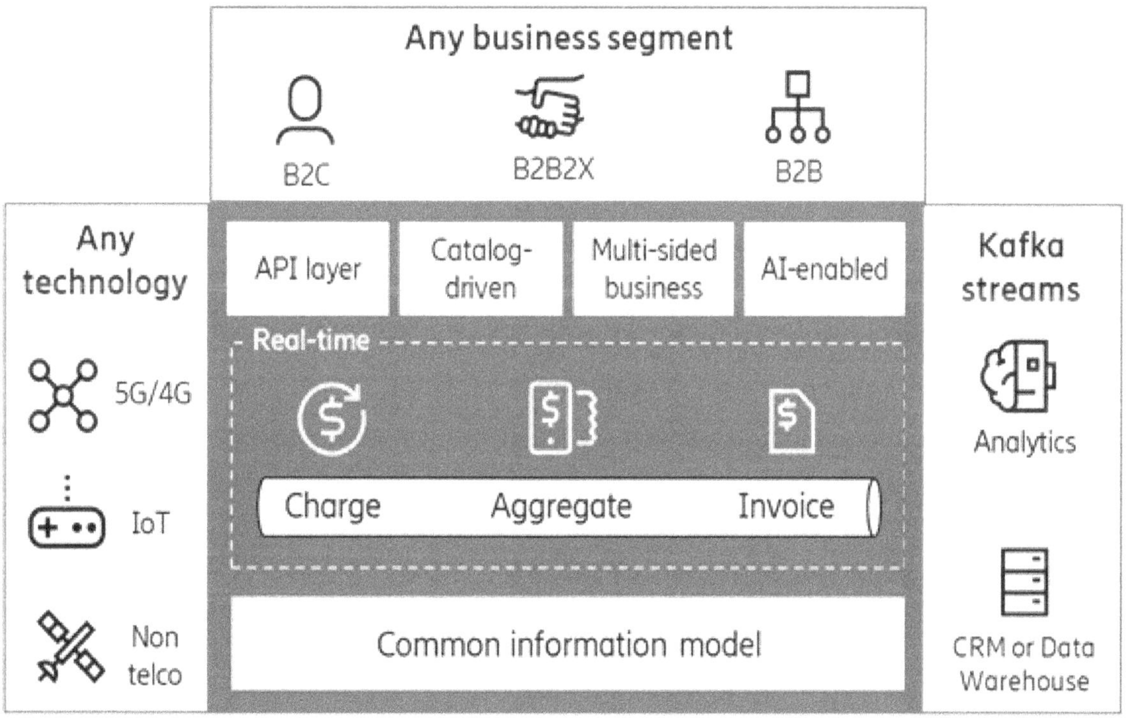

Figure 6.15: Conceptual View – Next-Gen Charging and Next-Gen Billing

Source: (Niemöller, 2022)

A converged intent aware Next-Gen Charging & Next-Gen Billing need to provide the following functionality:

- True convergence, centralized intelligence, and operations.

- Multi-sided business monetization, all in real-time: charge or bill based on any identifier.
- Business agility, AI-enabled: enables rapid service launches through a no-code/low-code approach and using configurable variation points.
- Intent aware with intent management functions capturing intent as well as reports for both charging and billing.
- Composable architecture, built-in APIs: modular, open digital architecture (ODA) with stateless service-based applications
- Cloud-native, automated, and resilient: microservices-based architecture
- Proven market leadership, trusted at scale.

Introduction of Intent to Next-Gen Charging and Billing enhances the monetization capabilities for operators. To explain this, consider a use case where customer intent is to prioritize 4K streaming between a specific time of the day for 2 hours daily with low latency.

In terms of delivering this intent, service layer translates the requirements to network slice intent with high bandwidth and low jitter, Next-Gen Charging applies premium price for the specified 2 hours and monitor QoS compliance, while the Next-Gen Billing issues real time adjustment or credits (some form of compensation) if QoS falls below threshold.

This would require intent reports capturing the delivered QoS to be reflected into Next-Gen Billing to be able to close the loop and trigger the compensation. On the other hand, Next-Gen Charging should be able to support negotiation of tariffs and service levels based on utility or priority values provided through intent metadata.

6.5 Challenges, Opportunities and Considerations

Together with the multiple opportunities presented by intent-driven networks, there are numerous challenges. Some of these aspects are considered below.

6.5.1 Challenges

1. Security

Security in intent-driven autonomous networks has two embodiments.

- **Intent for security:** This refers to the expression of security and privacy needs as intent requirements. These are customer and operator requirements for establishing security and privacy controls as part of service delivery.
- **Security for intent:** Intent requirements are critical assets that determine how the network is behaving.

Hence, it needs to be protected against unauthorized access. Securing the integrity of intent management refers to authorization of access to intent management, authorization to define and send certain

requirements and authorization of initiating actions that change the behavior of the networks. Furthermore, the integrity of intent needs to be protected.

2. Data

An intent management function needs to continuously monitor the fulfilment of intent requirements for identifying issues. This means it needs to observe data which includes configuration data as well as performance data. It also

needs to receive updates in line with use case needs. For example, it is not sensible to get updates about user latency several hours after the user made the experience, because then it may be far too late to take-action. Availability to data with the right observation schema can be a seen as a fundamental constraint to autonomous networks and intent capabilities. If a metric cannot be observed as needed, it is not suitable to be used in intent and related requirements cannot be made. This is also a direct factor for flexible charging and billing.

3. Trust

Why would an operator trust an autonomous network to make decisions and operate the network without direct human involvement? This is primarily a risk until the autonomous network has proven itself to make reasonable

decisions and manage risk correctly. Explainability will be a huge factor in gaining the trust of the operator. It refers to an autonomous network explaining and tracing its decisions so that humans executing their oversight role can verify the correctness. This might lead to handing over more responsibilities to the network and remove limiting policies and guardrails. Trust is also ensured by the flexibility of the intent-driven autonomous networks to move between different levels of autonomy from L3 to L4 and back, with “humans in the loops”, “humans on the loops” and “humans off the loops” based on demands and needs.

4. Conflict

Autonomous domains and their control functions including their IMFs take actions towards the network while they might be driven by different objectives. This leads to conflicts with actions towards conflict resolution. Conflicts must be detected, avoided or resolved where needed. Actions ideally become optimized across multiple objectives to

become a balanced compromise that is most preferential from business outcome perspective.

6.5.2 Opportunity

While there are challenges that needs to be addressed, it is evident that there are many opportunities for the taking in this transformative journey of Telco to Techco. One key ingredient to this would be customer centricity were experience would be at the center of everything, and the rich experience would be delivered with personalized and segmented/contextualized product and services.

Below are some foreseen business intents that could be considered as potential monetization opportunities:

- Real time SLA based charging for Network Slice
- Differentiated experience-based charging (QoS/QoE)
- Autonomous Drone and other such devices/machines
- Real time Event-Based Charging for B2B2X
- Intent based IoT Monetization
- Revenue share models, real time usage-based settlements

Also, T-Mobile and Meta can jointly unlock immersive AR/VR monetization—such as 4K VR concert streaming—by aligning Meta’s XR devices with T-Mobile’s intent-driven, low-latency 5G-Advanced network. By embedding QoE-based user intents (e.g., 4K, <50ms), T-Mobile can dynamically allocate resources, enable tiered pricing, and drive real-time, experience-based monetization.

6.5.3 Considerations

Rather than being disruptive, the transformation of the current BSS to intent ready BSS should be accomplished in multiple stages. The starting point could be the catalog simplification as that would directly impact the customer experience and would design and deliver new product and services for monetization.

It is no longer an option to create and maintain a localized set of product and services that exists as an alternative to dynamic offer creation. Hence it is critical to eliminate the catalog redundancies and fully comply to TMF SID modelling into a centralized product catalog that be used to compose and sell products using Open APIs.

Billing simplification is another vital piece of this transformation where offline rating/charging should be replaced with real-time rating, metering and monetization. The Billing function should be focused to manage billing, invoicing,

revenue recognition, financial settlements and collections. It should offload catalog, CDR management, offline rating functionalities to the purpose-built functions in the ecosystem.

By aligning with TM Forum's Open Digital Architecture (ODA) and leveraging TM Forum open APIs, a focused biller can operate within a decoupled framework. This approach ensures that each function manages specific data set with API access, enhances modularity, and improves operational visibility and compliance.

6.6 Chapter Summary

The future of telecommunications is being shaped by the following converging forces:

Simplification – how operators manage the ever-evolving complex networks. Instead of the traditional method where each action or service is manually configured, intent-based systems allow for a higher level

of abstraction where the system interprets what the customer wants to achieve and automatically manages the underlying complexity to fulfill that intent. This approach leverages AI, automation, and advanced analytics simplifying service delivery, reduce human interactions, minimize errors, and improve customer experience.

Differentiated Connectivity—what operators sell, tailored to the needs of consumers and enterprises. Differentiated connectivity refers to the capability of service providers to offer multiple levels of tailored connectivity services that meet the distinct and often varied performance requirements of emerging consumer and enterprise applications.

By ensuring deterministic performance, these services drive digital transformation, fostering richer consumer applications and advanced enterprise solutions, and fueling revenue growth. There are multiple steps in the journey, with network slices available today, and coming soon network APIs will allow for

Operators to capture new revenue streams from the wider developer ecosystem.

Autonomous Networks—how those services are delivered, with precision and intent. Autonomous

networks is a journey towards zero-touch networks that are self-optimized and healing to deliver a zero- trouble user experience. It uses end-to-end AI-powered intent driven, with a closed loop service assurance covering business intents, service intents, and resource intents as seen within the programmable network. In a fully autonomous network, the system has closed-loop automation capabilities across multiple services, multiple domains, and the entire lifecycle via cognitive self-adaption. The Journey to an autonomous

network with will increase business agility and enable multiple go-to-market models as services can be quickly provisioned and assured without human intervention.

Together, these redefine the context in which operators operate and demand a reimagining of BSS.

By treating charging and billing rules as machine-readable intents, which are validated, deployed, and assured in the same closed loop as QoS and QoE, operators can launch sophisticated 5G/6G business models (B2B, B2B2X) in minutes, price them dynamically, and ensure that revenue aligns with the service promise.

This intent-driven approach transforms BSS from a back-office system into a strategic enabler of growth; thus, empowering operators to monetize outcomes, deliver on customer expectations, and lead in the era of autonomous, experience-centric networks.

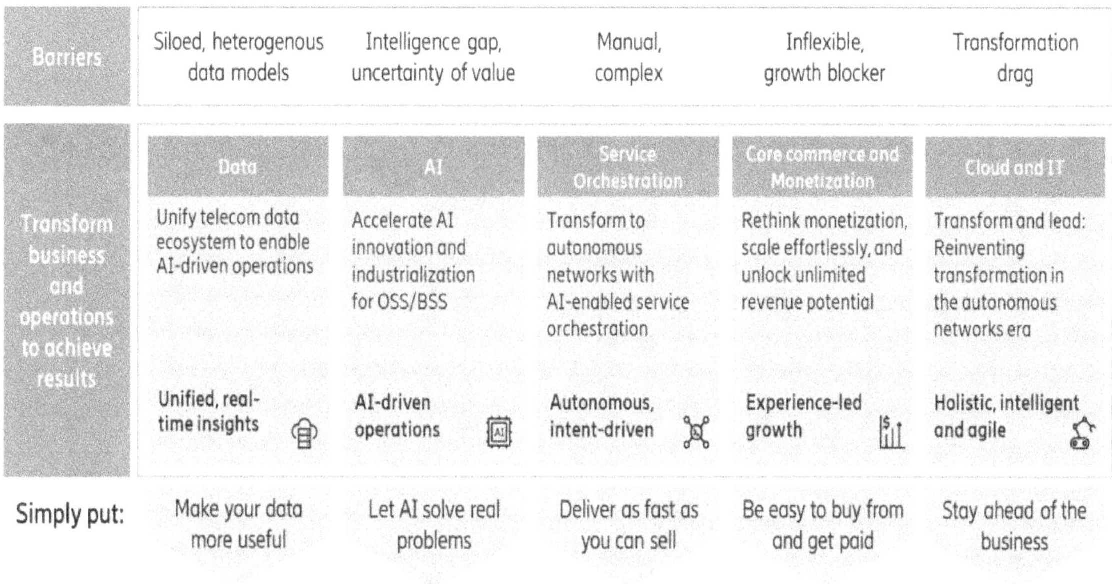

Figure 6.16: AI-Driven Telecom Transformation Framework for Business and Operational Outcomes

Very Short Questions

1. What is a dynamic product catalog?
2. Name the three layers of an autonomous network.
3. Define intent in the context of autonomous networks.
4. What is the main function of BSS in telecom operators?
5. Why is trust a critical factor in autonomous networks?
6. Give one example of a use case for intent-driven monetization.
7. What role does AI play in intent-based networks?
8. What is a closed control loop in intent management?
9. How does intent-driven monetization differ from traditional monetization?
10. What is the purpose of intent management functions (IMF)?

Short Questions

1. Explain the difference between "intent for security" and "security for intent."
2. Mention two TM Forum APIs used for product and service management.
3. How does intent-based provisioning enhance subscriber management?
4. How does 5G/6G influence BSS transformation?
5. List one challenge and one opportunity in intent-driven networks.
6. Why is cross-domain collaboration important in autonomous networks?
7. How are service intents translated to resource-layer requirements?
8. What is the significance of real-time charging in Next-Gen BSS?
9. What are the primary responsibilities of the Business Layer in intent-driven networks?
10. How does intent abstraction simplify network operations?

MCQs (Multiple Choice Questions)

1. **Which layer in an autonomous network is responsible for strategic business objectives?**
   A. Resource Layer
   B. Service Layer
   C. Business Layer
   D. Operations Layer
2. **Which organization defines intent ontologies for product and service management?**

A. IEEE
B. TM Forum
C. IETF
D. ISO

3. **Why is trust important in autonomous networks?**
   A. To increase bandwidth
   B. To allow operators to rely on autonomous decisions
   C. To reduce latency
   D. To manage the product catalog
4. **What is an example of intent-driven monetization?**
   A. Fixed monthly billing
   B. 4K VR concert streaming with tiered pricing
   C. Offline CDR rating
   D. Static network slices
5. **What does Next-Gen Billing enable in intent-driven networks?**
   A. Static charging
   B. Real-time adjustment based on QoS/QoE
   C. Manual invoice generation only
   D. Hardware provisioning
6. **What is the purpose of Intent Management Functions (IMFs)?**
   A. To replace AI in networks
   B. To coordinate autonomous operation based on intents
   C. To manage hardware only
   D. To perform manual billing
7. **What is the role of a closed control loop in intent management?**
   A. To predict future stock prices
   B. To detect deviations and act autonomously
   C. To manually configure resources
   D. To write network code
8. **Which is NOT a capability of a dynamic product catalog?**
   A. Real-time product adaptation

B. On-demand product generation

C. Manual-only product updates

D. Product retirement and replacement

9. Which of the following supports autonomous decision-making?

A. Agentic AI architecture

B. Paper-based logs

C. Offline billing only

D. Static network rules

10. What does BSS primarily manage in telecom networks?

A. Only network hardware

B. Products, orders, revenue, and customer relationships

C. AI algorithms

D. Security protocols

MCQ Answer sheet

Q1	Q2	Q3	Q4	Q5	Q6	Q7	Q8	Q9	Q10
C	B	B	B	B	B	B	C	A	B

Bibliography

Anglen, J. (2025). *AI agents for Network Configuration and Management*. Rapid Innovation.

Blueplanet. (25 C.E.). *What is Service Lifecycle Automation?* https://www.blueplanet.com/resources/what-is/what-is-service-lifecycle-automation

Cyril, H. P. (2025). Serialization of Telecom Provisioning Transactions in Distributed Systems. *International Journal of Current Engineering and Technology*, *15*(6), 526–533.

Dziuma, R., & Dyyak, R. (2020). *How to implement microservices in telecoms effectively*. N-IX. https://www.n-ix.com/implement-microservices-in-telecoms-effectively/

Freebie. (2025). *Nomad Logo PNG Transparent*.

Heindel, L. E., & Schlieber, K. J. (2002). Open architecture telecommunications provisioning systems. *Proceedings of Phoenix Conference on Computers and Communications*, 447–453. https://doi.org/10.1109/PCCC.1993.344514

Jamnadass, R. (2021). *Automation in the Telecoms Industry: A Key Differentiator*. 1–5.

Mazumder, S. (2022). *Telecom Microservices*. Aerospike. https://aerospike.com/blog/telecom-microservices/

Niemöller, J. (2022). *Business Success Factors of Autonomous Networks*.

Prakash, T. A. (2022). *WTH is Docker, and why do I need it?* Med. https://blog.devgenius.io/wth-is-docker-and-why-do-i-need-it-1f76deb827f9

Spenza. (2025). *TaaS vs. Traditional Telecom: Which is Right for Your Business?* https://spenza.com/telecom/taas-vs-traditional-telecom/

Yalamanchili, H. (2019). *Kubernetes at Earnest*. Medium. https://medium.com/earnest-engineering/kubernetes-at-earnest-984293e7e88c

ABOUT THE AUTHORS

Henry Cyril is a telecommunications systems architect and researcher recognized for his contributions to large-scale provisioning platforms, OSS/BSS modernization, and AI-driven cloud-native architectures for next-generation networks. His work centers on designing high-throughput, event-driven provisioning frameworks that enable deterministic transaction orchestration, large-scale subscriber migrations, and resilient operations across distributed telecom environments.

He has played a key architectural role in national-scale transformation initiatives, developing platforms capable of processing millions of provisioning transactions with strong consistency, fault tolerance, and automation. His expertise spans distributed systems engineering, concurrency control, transaction serialization, AI-driven anomaly detection, self-healing architectures, and intent-based orchestration aligned with evolving 5G and emerging 6G ecosystems.

Henry has authored multiple peer-reviewed journal publications in telecom provisioning and autonomous network operations. His research integrates applied mathematical modeling, machine learning, and distributed systems principles to advance scalable, resilient, and intelligent telecommunications infrastructure.

Uday Poranki is a seasoned telecommunications technology leader with deep expertise in OSS/BSS modernization and digital transformation. He specializes in helping service providers evolve legacy systems into cloud-native, agile, and scalable platforms that enable faster service innovation and operational efficiency. Uday is recognized for his work in Intent-Based Provisioning, translating high-level business and network intents into automated, policy-driven service orchestration.

He also champions Closed-Loop Autonomy within Autonomous Networks, leveraging AI-driven analytics and automation to enable self-optimizing, self-healing network operations. Through strategic customer engagement and solution leadership, Uday drives next-generation network transformation initiatives that deliver measurable business value and long-term operational excellence.

www.ingramcontent.com/pod-product-compliance
Lightning Source LLC
LaVergne TN
LVHW060036210926
848481LV00013B/3880